The Life
and Death of
Anna Mae
Aquash

JOHANNA BRAND
The Life and Death of Anna Mae Aquash

James Lorimer & Company, Publishers
Toronto   1978

ISBN 0-88862-152-3 Cloth
     0-88862-153-1 Paper

Design: Don Fernley
Cover illustration: Emma Hesse
6 5 4 3 2 1   78 79 80 81 82 83

Printed and bound in Canada

Canadian Cataloguing in Publication Data

Brand, Johanna, 1946-
   The life and death of Anna Mae Aquash

ISBN O-88862-152-3 bd.   ISBN 0-88862-153-1 pa.

1. Aquash, Anna Mae.   2. Indians of North America
- Canada - Biography.   3. American Indian
Movement. I. Title.

E78.C2B73   970'.004'97   C78-001054-X

James Lorimer & Company, Publishers
Egerton Ryerson Memorial Building
35 Britain Street
Toronto, Ontario

Contents

Acknowledgements

This book would not have been possible without help from many people.

Kevin Barry McKiernan generously shared research materials gathered during the four years he reported on the American Indian Movement for Minnesota Public Radio. In doing so he made important contributions to both content and accuracy.

John Deverell and Cathleen Hoskins provided editorial advice which I acknowledge with thanks. Thanks also to the Ontario Arts Council for a grant which made possible research and travel. So many individuals gave their time, support and hospitality that it would be impossible to acknowledge them all here. I am particularly grateful to Mary Lafford, Rebecca Julian, Ann Buttrick, Candy Hamilton, Mary Ann Brand and Marie Karklins. A special thanks goes to Ed Reed for his research assistance and helpful critiques throughout the course of my work and, more importantly, for his patient support and constant encouragement.

Throughout the course of my work I encountered the fear and suspicion that results from the phenomena this book attempts to describe. I also met, everywhere, courageous individuals who continued to work and speak out for what they believed in, often despite considerable personal hardship. It is to them that I dedicate this book.

J. B.
January 1978

Chronology

March 27, 1945: Anna Mae Pictou is born to Mary Ellen Pictou in Shubenacadie, Nova Scotia.

October 1962: Anna Mae moves to Boston, Massachusetts with Jake Maloney.

June 1964: Anna Mae gives birth to her first daughter, Denise.

September 1965: Anna Mae gives birth to her second daughter, Deborah. Anna Mae and Jake Maloney marry.

1968: The American Indian Movement (AIM) is founded in Minneapolis, Minnesota.

1970: Anna Mae and Jake Maloney are divorced. She becomes active in the Boston Indian Council.

Thanksgiving Day, 1970: AIM and eastern Indian supporters take over the *Mayflower II.*

February 1972: AIM demonstrates on behalf of Raymond Yellow Thunder, an Oglala Sioux killed in Gordon, Nebraska.

October 1972: AIM and other Indian groups organize the Trail of Broken Treaties Caravan to Washington, D.C. and then occupy the headquarters of the Bureau of Indian Affairs there.

November—December 1972: Oglala Sioux councillors attempt unsuccessfully to impeach Pine Ridge Reservation tribal chairman Richard Wilson.

January 1973: Wesley Bad Heart Bull is murdered in Custer, South Dakota. AIM organizes a demonstration which results in a violent confrontation with police and destruction of property.

February 1973: The Oglala Sioux Civil Rights Organization (OS-CRO) again attempts to impeach Pine Ridge tribal chairman Richard Wilson and fails. The organization invites AIM onto the troubled reservation.

February 27, 1973: OSCRO and AIM supporters begin a 71-day occupation of the village of Wounded Knee.

April 1973: Anna Mae and Nogeeshik Aquash journey to Wounded Knee and are married there on April 12.

May 8, 1973: The Wounded Knee occupation ends. Douglass Durham begins his association with AIM.

Autumn 1973: AIM leader Dennis Banks goes underground to

escape imprisonment and eventually flees to the Northwest Territories. He returns to the United States with the assistance of Douglass Durham.

January 8, 1974: The trial of Dennis Banks and Russell Means on charges arising from the occupation of Wounded Knee begins in St. Paul, Minnesota.

Summer 1974: Anna Mae and Nogeeshik Aquash separate, and she begins full-time work with AIM in Minneapolis-St. Paul.

August 1974: Ojibway warriors occupy Anicinabe Park, near Kenora, Ontario, and Dennis Banks and Douglass Durham are called in to mediate the dispute.

September 12, 1974: Charges against Dennis Banks and Russell Means are dismissed because of government misconduct in the trial proceedings.

September—October 1974: The Native People's Caravan reaches Ottawa.

October 10, 1974: Los Angeles cab driver George Aird is murdered, and AIM members Skyhorse and Mohawk are later charged with the crime.

January 1, 1975: The Alexian Brothers' Novitiate near Gresham, Wisconsin is occupied and held for one month by the Menominee Warrior Society.

March 12, 1975: Douglass Durham confesses he is an FBI spy.

January—June 1975: There is an increase of violence and murder on the Pine Ridge Reservation.

June 26, 1975: FBI agents Coler and Williams are shot to death near Oglala. The FBI invades the Pine Ridge Reservation.

September 5, 1975: Anna Mae Aquash and six others are arrested in an FBI raid on the Rosebud Reservation.

November 14, 1975: Anna Mae and three others are arrested after a shoot-out on an Oregon highway.

November 24, 1975: Anna Mae returns to South Dakota to appear in court and is released into the custody of her attorney. She goes underground.

December 1975: Suspected of spying for the FBI, Anna Mae is brought to Rapid City, South Dakota for questioning by AIM.

December 20, 1975: Anna Mae, in California, makes her last known contact with friends in the Midwest.

January 16, 1976: Dennis Banks, a fugitive since August 1975, is arrested in California.

February 6, 1976: Leonard Peltier and Frank Blackhorse are arrested near Hinton, Alberta. Peltier requests political asylum in Canada.

February 24, 1976: The body of Anna Mae Aquash is found near Wanblee, South Dakota.

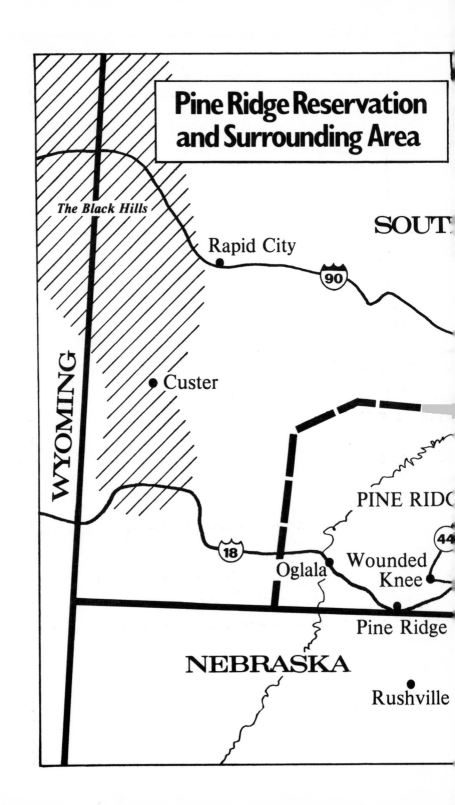

Pine Ridge Reservation and Surrounding Area

The Black Hills

SOUT

Rapid City

90

WYOMING

Custer

PINE RIDG

44

18

Wounded
Knee

Oglala

Pine Ridge

NEBRASKA

Rushville

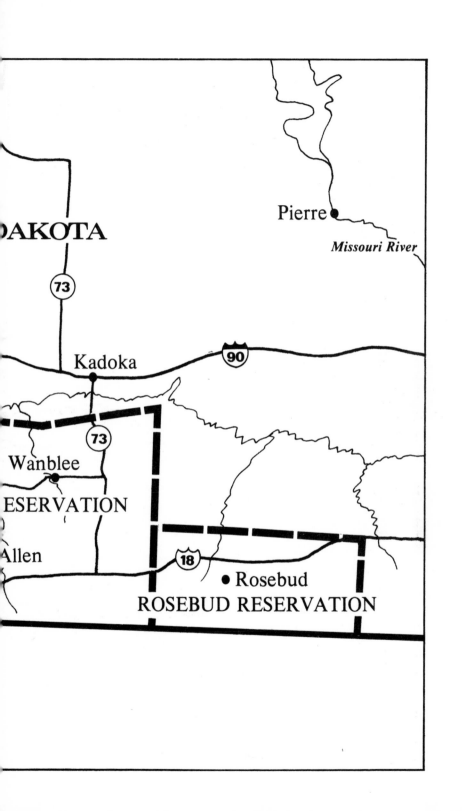

1/Just Another Dead Indian

The weather in the village of Wanblee, South Dakota, was unseasonably mild on February 24, 1976. Roger Amiotte was taking advantage of the unexpected thaw to build a fence on a rugged section of land he had recently added to his 2,500-acre ranch on the Pine Ridge Indian Reservation.

The Amiotte spread straddles the northeast boundary of the three-million-acre reservation, at a point where rolling, grassy hills give way to the sandy buttes and semi-arid terrain of the South Dakota badlands. An hour's drive to the southwest is the village of Wounded Knee, built on the site where hundreds of Sioux followers of Chief Big Foot were massacred by the United States Army in 1890. An hour to the northeast is the South Dakota state capital, Pierre. Two hours to the northwest are Rapid City and Mount Rushmore in the Black Hills, ancient Indian sacred ground.

Highway 73 runs north from the eastern edge of the reservation toward its border but first winds by the Amiotte trailer home and down a long hill, snaking among the jagged buttes. At the bottom of the hill, on the western edge of the pavement, is a shoulder just wide enough to park a car. Just after 2 p.m. on February 24, Amiotte was working his way along a dry creekbed paralleling this part of the highway at a distance of about 100 yards, concealed from the view of passing traffic by a steep, 30-foot embankment.

Suddenly the rancher spotted a human corpse curled up at the base of the precipice. He went no closer but drove immediately to his trailer home and phoned the disturbing discovery to the police dispatcher in the village of Pine Ridge, 100 miles to the southwest.

The police came quickly: sheriff's deputies from the nearby town of Kadoka, Bureau of Indian Affairs (BIA) police from Wanblee, FBI agents and more BIA police from Pine Ridge. Within two hours at least ten law enforcement officials had appeared to inspect the body and examine the site.

What they saw was the body of a young Indian woman, lying on her left side, knees slightly drawn up. She was wearing a light-coloured shirt, dungarees and an off-red ski jacket. The fingernails were long and there was a large turquoise bracelet on her right arm. The police searched exhaustively and took photographs, but found only a hair clasp at the top of the embankment and bits of hair here and there down its face, indicating the woman had gone off the cliff. The woman's clothing was intact and there were no apparent signs of a struggle or foul play. She carried no identification of any kind.

At about 4:30 p.m. when the police had completed most of their work, Jim Charging Crow, the old ambulance driver from Wanblee, and his wife drove the body to the village of Batesland where it was transferred to another vehicle and taken the remaining distance to the Public Health Service Hospital in Pine Ridge village.

Steven Shanker, the young doctor on duty, found the body quite decomposed. Upon removing some of the clothes he suspected immediately that death was not by natural causes and that the Indian woman had a fractured skull. When he turned the head, Shanker observed that the hair was matted with blood and a considerable amount of blood came off on his plastic gloves. He told a nurse to notify the police but did not examine the body further, sending it instead to the refrigerated morgue. "I didn't go further because the smell was bad, and I assumed a thorough post mortem would be done. I thought it was a police matter," he later explained. Night duty nurse Inez Hodges, fearing that the dead woman might be her missing roommate, briefly examined the body in the morgue and got a handful of blood when she turned the head. She did not recognize the corpse.

The pathologist under contract with the BIA to perform autopsies at Pine Ridge was Dr. W.O. Brown of Scottsbluff, Nebraska. Notified of the case the evening of February 24, Dr. Brown flew to the reservation in his private airplane and proceeded to the hospital at about noon of the following day. He conducted his examination, deciding that the case was "awfully routine"; so routine, in fact, that he had X-rays taken only of the woman's dental plate, not of her entire body. One of the chemical tests Brown did indicated that the dead woman had had sexual intercourse not long before her death. The pathologist noted a large abdominal scar due to previous gall bladder surgery and bodily markings that indicated at least one pregnancy.

Except for a small cut on the head, however, Brown reported no evidence of physical injury. He concluded that the woman had died of exposure and had been dead about two weeks and speculated that, like many other reservation residents over the years, she had gotten drunk, fallen asleep and frozen to death. Laboratory analysis later revealed no alcohol or drugs in the woman's blood.

Before ending his perfunctory performance, however, Dr. Brown took an unusual measure. He cut the woman's hands from the body at the wrists, placed them in a preserving jar and turned them over to one of the FBI agents observing the proceedings.

Officially, the unidentified woman died of exposure. Her body was returned to the morgue. Hospital dentist, Bill Moss, checked Dr. Brown's X-rays of the teeth against the dental records of a number of persons known to be missing, but without result. Police showed photographs of the dead woman's face and clothing to at least one person who had reported a missing female relative. Two relatives of Myrtle Poor Bear from the reservation town of Allen, South Dakota visited the morgue to see if she were the "dead-on-arrival" from Wanblee. A squib in the *Rapid City Journal* stated simply that the body of an unidentified woman had been found near Wanblee. No notice or description of the body was posted in any prominent place. On the reservation the normally vigorous gossip and interest in seeing who is dead was sharpened by remarks from hospital staff sceptical about the autopsy findings. There seemed to be no intensive effort by police to have the body viewed and identified.

The body remained in the hospital morgue for five or six days. Dr. Shanker said he tried to keep people out of the morgue during that time. On Sunday, February 29, Elaine Quiver, a teacher in Pine Ridge, viewed the body at the hospital to determine if it were that of her cousin who had been reported missing. Sometime after that—there is no record of the date—the body was sent to a mortuary in Rushville, Nebraska, 25 miles south of Pine Ridge.

Tom Chamberlain, the aging mortician who does most of the reservation business, estimated he kept the body in his garage for no more than two days before it was buried. But Chamberlain kept no records; instead of the usual handwritten notations, he later clipped newspaper articles relating to the case into the record book.

By the time the corpse arrived in Rushville, enbalming was out of the question, and Chamberlain placed it in his garage—his only cool storage facility—and sprinkled it with a strong-smelling disinfectant powder. This arrangement he judged perfectly satisfactory for preventing further decomposition, given the winter weather. To his surprise, he soon received orders from the BIA to proceed with the burial. Reservation Police Chief Ken Sayres, claiming to be worried about further decomposition, arranged for the reservation welfare office to authorize the funds for a pauper's burial.

At this point, Tom Chamberlain had neither an official death certificate nor a burial permit for the body. "It was the darndest thing I ever saw," he said later. "I've been doing this for over 50 years and haven't run into a case like this yet." He thought there was no compelling reason for the hasty burial of the as-yet unidentified body; in his long career he'd seen many more badly decomposed bodies and he said the body could have stayed in his garage as long as the weather remained cold.

Chamberlain had some problems finding a church and cemetery that would bury the woman without the usual documents, but finally Father Joseph Sheehan, the aged priest at Holy Rosary Mission near Pine Ridge village, consented to perform the task. Burial of the dead, he said, was one of the seven corporal works of mercy. Again no records were kept. Father Sheehan believes he performed the short Catholic ceremony on Ash Wednesday, March 3, 1976. But his altar boys say it took place on Shrove Tuesday, March 2. There were further difficulties when the rough box containing the coffin proved too large for the prepared grave, and it had to be made larger by hand digging on the morning of the funeral. With a few brief prayers and blessings the deed was done.

Little more than a week after its improbable discovery, the body of the young Indian woman lay beneath the cold, snowy ground in an unmarked grave. A few days later, on the evening of March 6, radio and television broadcasts announced that fingerprint analysis by the FBI in Washington, D.C. had, on March 3, identified the "dead-on-arrival" from Wanblee as Anna Mae Pictou Aquash.

The news sent shockwaves rippling through the reservation. Anna Mae Aquash, a Micmac Indian from Nova Scotia, was a well-known activist in the American Indian Movement and a close friend of prominent AIM leaders Dennis Banks and Leonard Peltier. She was a veteran of the 1973 Wounded Knee occupation and of many subsequent AIM actions. Since November 25, 1975 she had been a fugitive from the FBI. The Pine Ridge Reservation had been in a state of violent political turmoil ever since 1973; many local AIM supporters had been terrorized and some had been killed. That a national AIM organizer, whose home was not on the reservation, should be found dead of exposure on a lonely stretch of reservation highway was more than unlikely—it was bizarre.

Some Pine Ridge Reservation residents had learned before the public announcement that Anna Mae might be the "dead-on-arrival" from Wanblee. Early on the morning of March 6, Candy Hamilton, a worker with the Wounded Knee Legal Defence/Offense Committee (WKLDOC)—an AIM support group organized during the Wounded Knee occupation—received an unusual telephone call from St. Paul, Minnesota. RCMP officers had visited Anna Mae's relatives in Nova Scotia and Ontario, saying that she was the person found near Wanblee, the caller reported. Hamilton was asked to confirm and supply further information.

When she called BIA police chief Ken Sayres to ask if the dead woman had been identified, Hamilton received a peculiar response. "Sayres said there was no positive identification and that they were still checking out a number of leads from out of state." Proceeding cautiously because Anna Mae Aquash was a fugitive, Hamilton asked if the police were checking leads from out of the country. Chief Sayres ignored the question. He did supply a description of the dead woman, however, which bore no resemblance to the woman Hamilton knew. Sayres said that the dead woman was about 25 years old, five feet six inches tall and was wearing tennis shoes and a red ski jacket.

Candy Hamilton, who had no reason to believe that Anna Mae had been on the Pine Ridge Reservation, was encouraged by this exchange. Aquash was just over five feet tall; she was too sensible to wear tennis shoes in the middle of winter; and Chief Sayres had said nothing about the distinctive rings, bracelet or medicine pouch which she always wore. Hamilton's hopes were dashed, however, by the official public announcement of the identification later the same day.

Chief Sayres' equivocation was only the first of many stumbling blocks Anna Mae's friends encountered in their efforts to learn what had happened to the body following its discovery. That, and their knowledge of Anna Mae Aquash heightened their suspicions that there was something amiss with the official story. Anna Mae's sister, Mary Lafford, fearing that no one in South Dakota would pursue the investigation further, called from Nova Scotia to insist that the body be shipped to Canada immediately. She relented only when Hamilton persuaded her that the matter would not be dismissed. Anna Mae's friends knew she never walked or travelled alone on the reservation; that she did not frequent the Wanblee area; and that she certainly would not have been hitch-hiking alone on a desolate highway ten miles from that settlement. They also knew she did not drink or take drugs.

By early Sunday, March 7, Candy Hamilton and others had learned of Anna Mae's welfare burial and they went to confirm the location of the grave in Holy Rosary Cemetery. Hamilton was struck by the irony of the fact that her friend, a devout follower of traditional Indian religion who hated the Christian churches, had been buried in a Catholic ritual. On Monday morning Hamilton and two friends tried to see BIA police chief Ken Sayres, who was unavailable. They were unable to elicit much information from the BIA officer in charge: after each question posed by the women he crossed the hall to confer with FBI agents and returned with a reply. Finally, in frustration, he told the little group to speak to the FBI since they had handled the case. The agents, however, refused to answer any questions.

By this time the reservation was rife with rumours that Anna Mae Aquash had died violently. Gladys Bissonnette, an elderly

Oglala Sioux woman who would have recognized the dead woman, claimed she volunteered to look at the body when she was at the mortuary picking up the body of a relative. She said Tom Chamberlain refused to let her do so, telling her he was under "orders" to show it only to "authorized" persons. She claimed to have overheard Chamberlain telling an unidentified person on the telephone that he would not bury the body without identification or without approval from the state licensing office in Lincoln, Nebraska. Still other rumours said Chamberlain had been asked to bury the woman under an assumed name, which he also refused to do. Chamberlain denied all of these conversations. Rumours were also beginning to surface that the dead woman had an obvious head wound. Candy Hamilton used this information to persuade the WKLDOC support group in St. Paul to take action.

WKLDOC attorney Bruce Ellison, on Monday, March 8, sought an order to exhume the body for a second autopsy. He was surprised to learn that the FBI was already in the process of filing an affidavit for the same purpose in U.S. federal court. The FBI document offered three reasons: no X-rays had been performed during the first autopsy; Aquash might have been the "victim of a hit-and-run accident"; or she might have been killed "because AIM suspected her of being an informer". Ellison did not file the WKLDOC application, and the FBI agreed to postpone the exhumation until a pathologist representing the dead woman's family could be brought in from Minneapolis to observe the second autopsy. At the exhumation, Candy Hamilton spoke to two men who identified themselves as FBI agents. According to the gravediggers, prisoners from the Pine Ridge jail who had assisted at the burial, these same two men had also attended the original burial of Anna Mae's body.

The second autopsy was scheduled for March 11. That day a group of Anna Mae's friends, attorney Bruce Ellison and their pathologist, Dr. Gary Peterson, waited at length outside the Pine Ridge Hospital autopsy room for the FBI pathologist. Finally their enquiries revealed there would be no FBI pathologist; the Bureau planned only to take X-rays and if there were to be an autopsy, Dr. Peterson would have to do it. Unprepared to be more than an observer, the St. Paul pathologist had not brought his instruments. The hospital could not provide the necessary equipment, and he had to buy a kitchen knife in the local supermarket before he could begin his work.

The concerns of Anna Mae's family and friends were quickly vindicated: even before he began the detailed examination, Dr. Peterson noticed a bulge in the dead woman's left temple and dry blood in her hair. He turned the head and could see that the back of the head had been washed and powdered. An area of dark discoloration was visible at the base of the neck. Further investigation and the X-rays revealed a wound at the base of her skull, behind the right ear. The physician soon recovered what he judged to be a .32 calibre bullet accounting for the bulge in the temple. There were signs of powder burns around the wound in the neck. Dr. Peterson's conclusion as to the cause of death was unequivocal. Anna Mae Aquash had not died from exposure. She had died from a bullet shot at close range into the back of her head.

Some in the small group waiting outside the autopsy room were shocked by the news; others were less surprised. Over the last few years they had come to expect unsatisfactory explanations for the deaths of AIM supporters and it did not seem so remarkable that Dr. Brown examined Anna Mae Aquash and failed to find a bullet lodged in her skull. It was not until later, however, that it became clear just how superficial Dr. Brown's examination was.

During the original autopsy Dr. Brown requested no X-rays of the dead woman's head or body, although X-rays of her dental plate were taken. He later justified these omissions on the grounds that X-rays were "too time-consuming" and that the body was "stinky" and "decomposed". Dr. Brown's autopsy was further discredited by the rest of the second autopsy. His own report was not even filed until well after the second examination had taken place. "The organs are distributed somewhat randomly within the body cavity," Dr. Peterson wrote. What was left of the brain he found in the chest cavity. A number of organs, including the stomach, remained unopened and unexamined.

In his report, dated March 15, Dr. Brown claimed he had performed a full examination of the gastro-intestinal tract. "The G.I. appeared normal throughout, except for post mortem changes," the Nebraska physician wrote. "The stomach contained 100 cc's of dark bloody material of nondescript odour. There were post mortem changes in the gastric mucosa of a non-specific appearance. The appendix was present." Dr. Peterson found, to the contrary, that "the stomach is unopened and upon opening contains 5 cc's of mucoid reddish material.... The appendix cannot be identified."

Dr. Brown reported that the kidneys appeared normal on dissection and that the right kidney weighed 130 grams. Dr. Peterson found that the kidneys lay undissected in their respective kidney beds and that the right kidney weighed 160 grams. Moreover, Dr. Peterson did not agree with Dr. Brown's conclusion that the woman had been dead from ten days to two weeks at the time she was found. It would have been impossible to pinpoint the exact date or time of death, Dr. Peterson said, because of the fluctuating weather conditions; but it appeared to him that death had occurred at least three weeks—and possibly longer—before the corpse was found. While Dr. Brown had ruled out rape because he claimed there were no signs of physical violence, Dr. Peterson, who specializes in forensic rape, said rape could have occurred without any outward evidence of violence. Nor did Dr. Peterson rule out the possibility that the woman had been beaten, saying expert beatings can occur without leaving obvious bruises.

In apparent reply to the Peterson findings, Dr. Brown wrote in his autopsy report: "It is understood that a subsequent examination revealed a bullet wound of the head which I inadvertently overlooked. Although there were extensive post mortem changes in the brain, I found nothing in the examination of the brain to indicate involvement of this organ by the bullet track." The tendency of the brain to liquefy after death might support this defence were it not for other evidence of damage left by the bullet passing from the lower right to the upper left through the skull.

When questioned later about his autopsy, Dr. Brown was defensive and aggressive: "Everybody makes mistakes, haven't you ever made mistakes?" He characterized his failure to take X-rays as a "calculated risk". Although he had used the Pine Ridge Hospital X-ray equipment on other occasions, this time he found "it was too awkward". He insisted that "Anna Mae Aquash wasn't dead when she went off the cliff....Frostbite was the cause of death. The bullet may have initiated the mechanism of death, the proximate cause of which was frostbite."

"Why all the interest in this case?" he asked. "It seems awfully routine, you know. So they found an Indian body—so a body was found."

Dr. Brown estimated that he performed an average of 30 to 35 autopsies on the reservation each year, netting him earnings of about $20,000. When contacted three months after the autopsy, he did not know that his contract with the BIA had been cancelled. "I don't care whether they terminate it or not. Working conditions deteriorated to the point where going there is no fun any more."

Dr. Brown's failure to find a bullet lodged in the dead woman's temple may simply have been an oversight, as he claimed. The hurried amputation of the dead woman's hands may have been nothing more than the eagerness of authorities to identify the woman, notify her relatives and have her buried. The events that followed the discovery of the body of Anna Mae Aquash suggest, however, that there were other factors involved.

When Roger Amiotte reported the discovery of a body near Wanblee to the police dispatcher in Pine Ridge, the information produced a surprisingly large response. Among the lawmen who turned up at the site during the two hours before the body was removed were several FBI agents, including Donald Dealing and David Price; BIA police chief Ken Sayres and officers Doug Parisian, Nathan Merrick, James Stensgar, Paul Herman and Glen Little Bird; and Sheriff Helsell from nearby Jackson County and his deputies. One reason for this was the question of jurisdiction: the body was found close to the reservation border and it was not immediately clear whether the BIA or the Jackson County sheriff would take charge of the case.

The presence of the FBI was later explained by BIA Chief Ken Sayres to Shirley Hill-Witt, who was investigating the case for the United States Commission on Civil Rights. There had been so much violence on the reservation since Wounded Knee, he told her, that "it was usual procedure for the BIA on Pine Ridge to assume that all deaths were homicides". The issue of police jurisdiction on the reservation has always been contentious. During World War II the FBI was given responsibility to investigate 13 major crimes, including murder. The native people claim this jurisdiction violates the treaty which clearly designates the all-Indian BIA force responsible for law and order on the reserve.

More difficult to explain is the refusal of some of the law officers to admit that they were in fact on the scene. Chief Sayres, for example, denies he was present and claims that only BIA officers Merrick, Herman and Little Bird and FBI agent Donald Dealing were present. His omission of FBI agent David Price is significant.

The assistant special agent in charge of the FBI's Rapid City office, headquarters for agents who work on the reservation, is Norman Zigrossi. In the weeks and months that followed the discovery of Anna Mae Aquash's body, Zigrossi insisted that at first only one FBI agent had responded to the call. For a time he refused to name that agent, but later confirmed that it was Donald Dealing. Under repeated questioning, Zigrossi suggested that other agents may have gone to the scene out of curiosity.

National FBI Director Clarence Kelley told a similar story in a public statement on May 26, 1976 when he sought to clarify the FBI's role after the Aquash case had received widespread media attention. In a key portion of the statement, in which he described official response to Roger Amiotte's call, Kelley stated: "Within 20 minutes of the receipt of the report, officers of the BIA, accompanied by a special agent of the FBI *who had never had any personal contact with Ms. Aquash and who had never seen a photograph of her* arrived on the scene" [emphasis added]. Was this special agent Donald Dealing, the only agent whose presence at the scene FBI statements account for? If so, he covered the distance between Pine Ridge village and the location of Anna Mae's body near Wanblee—a distance of more than 100 miles—at impossible speed. Reports by BIA officers that Donald Dealing arrived at the scene at about 4:30 p.m. are obviously more plausible.

The FBI has refused to clearly indicate the number of agents on the scene when the body was found. Despite statements from BIA policemen naming David Price as one of the agents on the site, FBI officials have refused to acknowledge Price's presence. Price knew Anna Mae Aquash: he had arrested her once, recognizing her on sight, and had interrogated her then and on a previous occasion. Eyewitness reports placed Price at the morgue the day of the autopsy. Did he assist in photographing the body prior to the examination? If so, he could easily have identified the woman.

The FBI attributes Price's failure to do so to the state of the body. "One agent who helped photograph Ms. Aquash did know her from a previous contact but was not able to identify her because of decomposition of the body," FBI Director Kelley reported in his May 26 statement. Yet it is doubtful that the body was decomposed beyond recognition. Hospital workers who saw it when it was brought into the morgue the evening of February 25 claim that anyone who knew the woman could have recognized her. This claim is supported by Dr. Gary Peterson, who said the body "was not severely decomposed. I expected much worse decomposition." Furthermore, FBI photographs of the corpse were shown to persons who had reported missing relatives. All photographs of Anna Mae Aquash's face—photos taken at the site where the body was found and later—are now in the FBI's possession and the Bureau has refused to allow outsiders to see them.

Lawmen who were in and out of the autopsy room on February 25 have stated that two FBI agents, David Price and his partner at the time, William Wood, were present when Dr. Brown performed the first autopsy. However, Dr. Brown's report names only the BIA officers present. When questioned, he equivocated about the presence of FBI agents, first saying they may have been there, then denying it. The FBI continues to deny that any of its agents attended the first autopsy. Yet BIA police say that when Dr. Brown amputated the dead woman's hands he turned them over to either Price or Wood.

Agent Wood, in the affidavit filed to request the exhumation of the body, stated: "Due to decomposition of the body it was impossible to obtain fingerprints...*during the course of the autopsy...*" [emphasis added]. And in his statement, FBI Director Kelley asserts that "due to the difficulty of obtaining fingerprints at the scene...*an FBI agent suggested* that Dr. Brown could remove the hands..." [emphasis added]. Both statements would indicate that agents were present at the autopsy. Norman Zigrossi, head of the FBI's office in Rapid City, did admit much later that agents were at the hospital immediately before and after the examination. Thus the initial denial may simply be a matter of semantics. From eyewitness statements it seems clear that agents, including Price and Wood, had considerable opportunity to view the body and consult with Dr. Brown.

The contradictory nature of the various official statements becomes even more evident when attempts are made to determine who gave the order to sever the hands. Dr. Brown first claimed he had a court order from the U.S. Attorney and then denied such an order existed. The FBI claimed responsibility for the order while BIA police chief Ken Sayres said it had been his decision, made in consultation with the FBI, because at that point the entire case was under BIA jurisdiction. No explanation was given for why the hands were cut off within 24 hours of discovering the body, before relatives would even have had an opportunity to view it intact.

No attempt was made to take fingerprints, Chief Sayres said, for fear of destroying them. Had such efforts in fact been made it is likely they would have produced satisfactory results. When Dr. Gary Peterson examined the body on March 11, he also examined the severed hands, which the FBI had returned. His report states that all the fingers showed distinct fingerprint ridges although the finger pads appeared somewhat wrinkled. Peterson, who has performed more than 1,000 autopsies, said the fingertips were in a condition which would have yielded satisfactory results. Injection of fluid under the skin would have made fingerprints even more distinct.

Yet Pine Ridge officials made no attempt to obtain even a single fingerprint and decided instead to take an extreme course of action. Even in an extreme case, normal procedure would have been to sever the fingertips only, placing each in the appropriate finger of a rubber glove. This is exactly what was done in Washington as Dr. Peterson was able to observe on March 11.

Nor did Pine Ridge authorities make more than a perfunctory attempt to identify the body other than by its fingerprints. Anna Mae Aquash's height, her unusually small feet, her partial dental plate, gall bladder scar and distinctive jewellery—all would have helped to identify her if the information had been disseminated. And all should have made her recognizable to FBI agents who possessed detailed information about her.

Given these facts and the numerous irregularities in the official handling of the case, friends of Anna Mae Aquash began to speculate: was there some deeper significance to the unnecessary mutilation of the body? Was it intended that the severed hands not reach Washington and the body be left unidentified? There is support for the suspicion that identification was at least deliberately delayed. An FBI report on the matter to Canadian External Affairs Minister Donald Jamieson states: "In an effort to effect positive identification of the body, the hands were severed and forwarded to the FBI's identification division, Washington, D.C. *on March 3.*" [emphasis added]. Did seven days elapse between the time the hands were severed and the date they were sent to Washington and identified? AIM attorney Ken Tilsen charged later that the identification was purposely delayed. Tilsen speculated that it may have been intended that the hands not reach Washington and that the dead woman never be conclusively identified. He claims this FBI plan may have been thwarted by an agent who was new to Pine Ridge and not familiar with the usual FBI operations there. Tilsen suggests that this unsuspecting agent may have seen the jar containing the hands, and thinking his colleagues had forgotten about them, simply done his job and sent them off to the laboratory.

The available evidence indicates that the body of Anna Mae Aquash could and should have been identified on the same day it was discovered. The cause of death—murder—could and should have been established the next day. Instead, Anna Mae Aquash's body remained unidentified in the Pine Ridge Hospital morgue for approximately five days and was still unidentified by the time it was hastily buried two days later. By the time the FBI finally identified her on March 3, there was a pathologists's official verdict that she had died of exposure and the body was six feet underground.

In this light, Dr. Brown's failure to find the bullet, the hurried severing of the hands, the unexplained delay in identification, the hasty burial without benefit of identification, death or burial certificate all suggest something far more serious than casual and undisciplined police procedures. The evidence suggests a conspiracy to prevent the discovery and investigation of the murder of Anna Mae Aquash.

2/Wounded Knee, 1973

Dr. Gary Peterson's autopsy led to the inevitable conclusion that Anna Mae Aquash had been murdered. Almost as soon as he had concluded his work, lawyers for the Wounded Knee Legal Defence/Offense Committee charged that the FBI was perpetrating a cover-up either to hide its own involvement in the case or to protect the murderer. The charge resulted from more than the suspicious way in which Pine Ridge authorities had handled the Aquash murder: it grew out of the WKLDOC's three years of experience with law enforcement practices on the reservation.

Since the occupation of Wounded Knee, violence on the Pine Ridge Reservation had increased markedly. Incidents involving the death or injury of AIM members and supporters or the destruction of their property were rarely investigated thoroughly by either the BIA or the FBI, and charges were rarely laid.

When they learned that she had been murdered, Anna Mae Aquash's friends on Pine Ridge immediately suspected that she had been killed by one of the members of the reservation "goon squad" controlled by tribal chairman Richard Wilson. Even accepting Dr. Brown's estimate of the date of death, Anna Mae's death had probably occurred within days of the violent weekend of January 31, 1976 when the goons had moved into the village of Wanblee and fired on AIM supporters and their homes. Goons had firebombed one house while BIA police stood by watching. They fatally shot Byron De Sersa, grandson of the famed Sioux spiritual leader, Black Elk, after a high-speed car chase. Following that incident FBI agents in the village told De Sersa's friends, eyewitnesses to a murder, to "behave themselves". They arrested no one, although the names and addresses of De Sersa's attackers were well-known. Later one person was charged in connection with the crime, but only after he had turned himself in.

The Wanblee incident brought to a symbolic close the reign of terror that had accompanied Richard Wilson's four-year term as tribal chairman of the Pine Ridge Reservation. It was Wilson's election in the spring of 1972 that set the stage for the occupation of Wounded Knee a year later. The seizure of that tiny reservation settlement became a powerful symbol of modern American Indian resistance and set off a systematic campaign against the American Indian Movement. The United States Commission on Civil Rights, which investigated the Aquash and De Sersa murders, stated that many reservation residents felt that "they are the objects of a vendetta, and have a genuine fear that the FBI is 'out to get them' because of their involvement at Wounded Knee....."

The occupation of Wounded Knee, which began on February 27, 1973, brought to a head reservation grievances stemming from the treaty signed between the United States and the Sioux tribes at Fort Laramie in 1868. Again and again during the weeks of the occupation, the Oglala Sioux protesters and their AIM supporters insisted that they wanted to revert to the terms of that treaty. The 1868 accord was to have been a peace treaty between the U.S. and the Sioux. It provided the Sioux and Arapaho tribes with a reservation consisting of everything west of the Missouri River in present-day South Dakota, the area north of the Northern Platte River and east of the Big Horn Mountains—a reservation that took up half of the present-day states of South Dakota and Nebraska and one quarter of what are now the states of North Dakota, Montana and Wyoming. These were to be "unceded" Indian lands where no whites would pass through or settle. The Indians in turn agreed to give up their claims to other lands.

The treaty provided that if the reservation yielded less than 160 acres of farming land per person, the government would provide additional land. Anyone living on the reservation might own land privately; the remaining land was held in common by the tribe. The United States promised to provide schools and economic aid. An agent would live on the reservation and would forward complaints of treaty violation for prosecution. The United States government agreed to punish anyone, Indian or white, who violated the treaty.

In making the agreement, the chiefs and headsmen of the eight Teton Sioux tribes took into consideration both the practical and spiritual needs of their people. Included in the Great Sioux reservation were the Black Hills—"Paha Sapa" to the Indians. For generations the hills had been burial grounds for the great warriors of the Sioux nation, the place where the courageous Sundance was performed, the place where young warriors came on vision quests, the land where the Great Spirit dwelled. But the agreement also prevented trails across the hills which would divide and further diminish the great herds of buffalo, by then the principal source of sustenance for the nomadic tribes of the plains.

The 1868 treaty had not been in effect for long when rumours of gold in the Black Hills spread through the surrounding white communities. Miners looking for gold encroached on the Sioux land early in the 1870s. In 1874, General George Armstrong Custer led an exploratory expedition of 1,000 men into the Black Hills in contravention of the treaty. With him were miners, geologists, engineers and reporters. When gold was discovered on July 27, 1874, it was Custer who was most often credited with the discovery, not the prospector who actually found "the yella sand". Overnight Custer's name became a household word across America and roaring gold camps sprang up around what is now Custer, South Dakota.

Some historians say that Custer hoped to make his widespread fame the basis for a presidential bid in 1876, following what he thought would be an easy victory at the Battle of Little Big Horn. Instead, the Little Big Horn became the last military victory for the Sioux. Washington had responded to the Sioux protests over the armed invasion of their land in 1874 by sending a treaty commission to negotiate with the tribes for the Black Hills. After the Indians made it clear they had no intention of selling their remaining land, the United States passed a law forcing the sale and threatened to cut off rations to the tribes, to remove them to country south of the Arkansas River, to disarm them and take away their ponies. The forced sale of the Black Hills took place in 1876. Subsequent imposed agreements reduced the treaty lands from the guarantee of all the territory west of the Missouri to the five small and separate reservations that exist today.

But it was a new religious practice, the Ghost Dance, which prompted the final conquest of the Sioux. The new religion was basically passive, calling on the Indians only to dance: dancing would bring about a new world from which the white man would disappear and Indians would once again reign on a rejuvenated prairie. In the white communities, however, the dance inspired fear of renewed Indian rebellion. Lists were prepared in Washington naming those thought to be encouraging the outlawed ritual. Among the targets was Sitting Bull, who was assassinated when federal agents came to arrest him. Some of his Hunkpapa Sioux followers fled to the camp of the Minneconjou chief Big Foot, who himself was arrested a few days after Christmas 1890.

The cavalry troop that arrested that band was a reorganized unit of Custer's famous Seventh. It made camp at Wounded Knee, guarding the Sioux encampment with four Hotchkiss guns. While the scraggly band of Indians was being disarmed the following morning, a gun was discharged—some say accidentally— and a scrimmage followed between the soldiers and the poorly armed Indians. Many of the Indians fled, and as they did so the soldiers opened up with the big rapid-fire Hotchkiss guns, killing, it is estimated, as many as 300 of the 350 men, women and children. The victims were buried in a huge common pit near which was built the Wounded Knee Catholic Church. Eighty-three years later an historical marker outside the village noted the Indians' "defeat" while another sign urged tourists to view "the mass grave".

The lost treaty lands became the subject of innumerable twentieth-century lawsuits. The U.S. federal government eventually recognized that many of the lands were ceded without just compensation and in direct violation of the 1868 treaty. In 1974 the federal courts authorized payment of $17 million plus interest at five per cent since 1877, for a total of $100 million to be paid for the seven million acres of the Black Hills. Federal charges for "payments on the claim"—rations of food, blankets and the like—reduced the proposed net payment to $4.5 million, less than one dollar per acre. The Sioux Treaty Council rejected that settlement as insufficient and said the tribe wanted land compensation. They knew that in addition to land value, mineral resources in the Black Hills were worth many hundreds of times more than the proposed monetary compensation. One Black Hills mine alone had yielded in excess of $500 million in gold.

The Sioux Treaty Council, established by the 1868 treaty as the tribes' governing body, was made up of traditional chiefs and headsmen, leaders who emerged from the large clan or kinship groups. Chosen on the basis of their ability to represent the interest of these groups, their power derived from those Indians who, as a result of the treaty land allotments, owned most of the land on the reservation.

In 1934 this traditional system of self-government was overturned when Congress passed the Indian Reorganization Act, which was ratified by a referendum of Pine Ridge residents. The IRA established a new system of government with an elected tribal council. The Treaty Council, in opposing the new system had advocated that the referendum be boycotted. At the urgings of the old chiefs, many Indians did not vote. As a result the new system was approved and became the only one recognized by Washington. While traditional power rested with the chiefs and headsmen, it was the elected tribal council through which funds were channelled into the reservation.

The passage of the IRA put reservation political power in the hands of the majority. Today on Pine Ridge the majority of the 14,000 reservation residents are the approximately 8,000 mixed bloods who own little land. As the numerical majority they have the votes to elect a tribal chairman. The traditional Oglala Sioux people, who own most of the reservation land and are the strongest defenders of Indian treaty rights, are in the minority, with no effective political voice. Yet, without them there would be no reservation. While the amount of Indian-owned land on the reservation continues to dwindle, traditional families still own about half of the three million acres. Another half million are owned by the tribe and the remaining one million by white ranchers.

Theoretically the tribal council represents all reservation residents, but in matters of economic development, it represents primarily the landless. The traditional landowners, whose title stems from the 1868 treaty, own their land in trust with the BIA and benefit little from the millions of dollars in federal funds that come onto the reservation each year through the tribal council.

As trustee, the BIA acts as the Indians' representative in any land transaction, but that agency often does not act in the best interest of the Indian landowner. Much of the Indian-owned land is leased to non-Indian ranchers. In 1973 some of it brought as little as 80 cents per acre per year, a price negotiated by the BIA. Private lending institutions are reluctant to deal with Indian landowners because the BIA must be a party to all financial transactions. Bureaucratic problems become even more complicated if the individual landowner wants to deal with another federal agency, because the BIA jealously guards its jurisdiction.

As a result, many of the traditional Oglala Sioux families are paradoxically poor: they own vast acreage, but lack the technical skills and financial resources to develop their land. Too poor to become ranchers themselves, many lose all access to their land by renting it to white ranchers. In consequence, traditional landowners are among the poorest of Pine Ridge residents, more than half of whom are unemployed. In the early 1970s, half of the reservation's residents had an annual income of less than $2,000 while one third lived on meagre welfare payments. Rations of food—known as commodities—for welfare recipients consist largely of white flour, lard and dried beans. It is not surprising that health problems are severe. Alcoholism, tuberculosis and pneumonia are widespread; the infant mortality rate is four times the U.S. national average and the suicide rate twice as high as among non-Indians. The available health care is of poor quality. Doctors who used to flock to the Public Health Service to avoid military service no longer do so since the elimination of the draft. The result has been a deterioration of the care provided by the Public Health Service hospitals on the reservations.

The two main employers on Pine Ridge Reservation are the tribal council and the BIA. There is little industry and most small businesses are owned by whites. Even tourists who come to see the mass grave at Wounded Knee leave little cash behind. All federal and state funds allotted to the Pine Ridge Reservation are controlled by the tribal council. This makes the post of tribal chairman an influential one, since he controls reservation jobs. While theoretically the reservation police are hired by the BIA, under many administrations—and particularly under Richard Wilson—the police and the tribal courts are controlled by the chairman. It is the 8,000 Indians of mixed blood, who own little land, who rely on this ever-changing spoils system for their livelihood.

When Richard Wilson assumed office in 1972, the first jobs available went to his friends and relatives. Wilson followers—among them the toughs known throughout South Dakota as the "goon squad"—got jobs with the BIA. His brother became head of the tribal waterworks and well-repair projects; his wife was made director of the Head Start program; his nephew became personnel director and another brother became a "tribal consultant" even though, it is alleged, he never came near the tribal offices.

Those who opposed Wilson did so at the risk of losing their jobs, and several did: Geraldine Janis, Della Starr and Roslyn Jumping Bull were fired from their positions and later sued the tribe. Buddy Lamont lost his job; later he was killed during the siege of Wounded Knee. If Wilson did not directly control a program or position, he was able to exert enough pressure on those who did to ensure that his candidates were appointed.

Richard Wilson was by no means the first tribal chairman to indulge in political patronage; nor was he the first suspected of diverting tribal funds to his own account. It was the extent of Wilson's alleged corruption that angered reservation residents and triggered fierce opposition. Charges of corruption had followed Wilson since his involvement with the Oglala Sioux Housing Authority some years before and during his term as tribal councillor. In 1972 Wilson allegedly bought the votes that elected him: he was said to be funded by white businessmen to whom he promised lucrative housing and liquor contracts.

Once in office, Wilson failed to hold constitutionally-required meetings, choosing instead to work through the tribal council's executive committee. While council by-laws state that any expenditure over $500 must be approved by the whole council, Wilson alone approved the purchase of such items as $200,000 worth of trailers and a $330,000 building now used as the tribal courthouse. Wilson did not keep books. Tribal accounts were in such a state that when they were audited late in 1973 it was impossible to determine the nature of the transactions that had occurred, and charges of corruption against Wilson could not be proved.

Under the 1934 Indian Reorganization Act, tribal government is supervised by and answerable to the BIA, but Richard Wilson's relationship with the BIA superintendent and area director was such that when he violated constitutional requirements, those who protested were ignored.

The first attempt to impeach Wilson was launched by three tribal councillors supported by many traditional Oglala Sioux in November 1972. That and two succeeding attempts failed when Wilson was allegedly successful in buying off the councillors who represented the constituencies that opposed him.

Wilson countered the mounting opposition by bolstering his goon squad and using it to terrorize his opponents. Those who supported the American Indian Movement became candidates for beating or shooting. Their houses and cars were riddled with bullets or firebombed and the goons operated seemingly unrestrained by the BIA police. Some BIA police officers were in fact Wilson supporters. It was in part to check the violence of the goons that the Oglala Sioux Civil Rights Organization (OSCRO), formed in January 1973, invited the American Indian Movement onto the reservation and again started impeachment proceedings against Wilson.

AIM, the organization to which OSCRO turned for support, originated in Minneapolis in the summer of 1968, primarily to deal with the problems of urban Indians. Some of its founders had met in prison, shared common histories and problems and determined to fashion a civil rights organization geared specifically to the needs of American Indians. Housing and education were the movement's original priorities, but it first gained notoriety by patrolling the streets of the south Minneapolis ghetto and monitoring police treatment of Indian people, to safeguard their civil rights against violation by the police and the courts.

The Indian activism of the 1970s, which resulted in the occupation of Wounded Knee, was to some extent an outgrowth of the consciousness raised by black civil rights and anti-war activists in the late 1960s and of the tactics they developed. But early in its existence, AIM developed an emphasis on traditional Indian spirituality, resulting from an association of AIM leaders and the Sioux spiritual leaders, including Leonard Crow Dog. AIM leaders were also quick to realize that the problems of urban Indians were in part an outgrowth of problems of the reservations. The increasingly popular movement rapidly expanded the base of its activities, gaining national prominence as the result of such actions as the takeover of the *Mayflower II* on Thanksgiving Day 1970, a symbolic reclamation of Indian rights.

Traditional treaty rights were pursued in such actions as the occupation of Alcatraz Island in San Francisco Bay and fishing rights sit-ins, where the struggle centred around the rights of Indians to fish unrestrained by the laws controlling non-Indian sportsmen. AIM actions were essentially non-violent and the organization quickly developed the ability to capture media attention.

AIM's first prominent demonstration directed at the problems of Pine Ridge Reservation Indians occurred early in 1972. Reservation Indians had long been used to an unequal standard of justice in the neighbouring communities, but they were particularly outraged by the death of Raymond Yellow Thunder in February of 1972, in Gordon, Nebraska, a town they frequented for shopping and entertainment. Yellow Thunder, 53, was beaten, then taken to the American Legion Hall where, stripped from the waist down, he was forced to "dance" for the partying Legionnaires.

Some days later he was found in a parked truck, dead of head injuries received during a beating. His attackers were convicted on reduced homicide charges and received light prison sentences.

At the time, a number of native American groups, among them the American Indian Movement, were attending a policy and goals conference in Omaha, Nebraska. News of the case sent caravans of AIM cars rallying across the state line into Pine Ridge. Suddenly the colourless reservation streets were marked by licence plates from across the country, buttons, bumper stickers, red headbands and the sound of AIM drummers. Signs of "Red Power" were everywhere. A thousand demonstrators descended on Gordon to protest the Yellow Thunder killing and the lenient treatment of his attackers. Sherriffs' deputies from dozens of Nebraska towns mobilized in Gordon to bolster local law enforcement. The state highway patrol sent every available unit, and FBI agents and Nebraska Crime Bureau officials also converged on the scene.

There was no violence. Instead, town officials agreed to meet with Indian leaders to discuss grievances, many of which local Indians had been afraid to voice. The Gordon police chief, who for years had been accused of discriminatory law enforcement against Indians, was dismissed in a major concession to the demonstrators. Other promises were made, task forces established and study groups organized. It was a victory for AIM that gained it new respect among reservation residents. But, as memories of the dramatic confrontation dimmed, life for Indians in the Gordon area returned to what it had been.

In the summer of 1972, AIM, joined by a number of other Indian organizations, led a march on Washington, D.C. that was designed to call attention to problems on reservations, the violation of treaty rights and dissatisfaction with the BIA. The Trail of Broken Treaties demonstration took place just before the 1972 presidential election and led to the occupation of the BIA headquarters building. The occupation was unplanned, Indian leaders claimed, but necessary since the marchers were unable to obtain the accommodation they had been promised. Action threatened by riot police prompted the occupiers to barricade and fortify the building. The occupation is now remembered more for the damage to the BIA building than for the 20-point proposal the marchers submitted to the government. The proposals covered such issues as housing and educational and legal reforms and demanded the abolition of the BIA. While there were promises that White House officials would study the proposals, they were virtually ignored.

AIM considered the action a victory, although the organization was severely criticized for the property damages and the $60,000 "return home" fund given the protesters through an arrangement worked out by the White House. More established Indian organizations were quick to condemn AIM's confrontation tactics.

When AIM announced that it would hold a victory celebration on Pine Ridge following the Washington demonstration, tribal chairman Richard Wilson quickly bolstered his goon squad. A tribal council resolution calling on AIM to abide by reservation law was rewritten in the minutes to give Wilson wide powers with which he hired more goons, obtaining funds with the cooperation of local BIA officials. The antagonism between AIM and Wilson sharpened.

AIM staged another demonstration to protest the lenient treatment of the murderer of Wesley Bad Heart Bull in January 1973. The Oglala Sioux youth had been stabbed by a white man in a Custer, South Dakota bar. Authorities first took no action, then laid a charge of second-degree murder. AIM demanded a first-degree murder charge. But, unlike the Gordon demonstration a year earlier, this protest resulted in a bloody confrontation with police on the steps of the Custer courthouse. In the melee that followed, dozens were injured, including the dead youth's mother, Sarah Bad Heart Bull. The local chamber of commerce building was burned to the ground and fire damaged the courthouse, some automobiles and a gas station.

The confrontation led AIM to seek improved treatment of Indians in all the western South Dakota towns, but particularly in Rapid City where there is a fairly large Indian community. Amidst the tension following the Custer incident, meetings took place between AIM and local officials. By mid-February, there was a sizeable contingent of AIM members in Rapid City.

Meanwhile, tribal chairman Richard Wilson came under increasing pressure on the reservation. Three attempts to impeach him were thwarted. The Oglala Sioux Civil Rights Organization made a fourth attempt to impeach Wilson early in February 1973 and a hearing was slated for February 14. To prepare for that hearing Wilson called on the United States Marshals Service for support. By mid-February about 75 specially-trained marshals had arrived in Pine Ridge, ostensibly to protect the BIA building. They sandbagged the red brick office and set up a machine gun on the roof.

Wilson postponed his own impeachment hearing for another week. During that time high-level officials in the FBI, the BIA and the Marshals Service arrived on the reservation. Logistic support was provided by the Pentagon, working through the police agencies to disguise its involvement. At a February 22 meeting it was decided that Wilson should come to trial, but the trial date was set for the very next day, catching the OSCRO unprepared. For all practical purposes, Wilson presided at his own impeachment hearing. Naturally, he was not removed from office, and the outrage among his opponents increased.

With legal channels for change effectively blocked, the OSCRO group—whose membership totalled about 800 persons prior to the Wounded Knee occupation—faced the choice of submitting to Wilson's rule or challenging it by direct action. Thus, on the evening of February 27, 1973, the OSCRO met at Calico Hall, a small log building outside Pine Ridge village to discuss the refusal of both tribal and BIA officials to deal with their grievances. AIM leaders Russell Means, whose home is in the Porcupine district of the reservation, and Dennis Banks, a Chippewa Indian from Minnesota, were at the meeting. Also attending were the traditional chiefs and headsmen from all eight reservation districts.

Plans had been made for a dance and powwow after the meeting, but frustrated and angry Indians filled the tiny community hall to overflowing and in the end there were no festivities. Instead, those at the meeting got into their cars, formed a caravan and drove to Wounded Knee, 25 miles on the other side of Pine Ridge village. They seized the white-owned trading post and the wood-frame Catholic Church in the name of the Oglala Sioux. Eleven persons were taken hostage, including the trading post owners and a clergyman. Eventually a list of demands was drawn up.

Official response was quick; within hours, scores of heavily armed, specially-trained federal agents set up roadblocks cutting off all access to the village. Months of peaceful protest had yielded no results, but with this one act, the Oglala Sioux's grievances were front-page news. Suddenly, they were being heard not only by tribal and BIA officials, but by the entire nation.

On March 1, 1973, the *New York Times* quoted AIM leader Carter Camp, summing up the goals of the occupation: "We will occupy this town until the government sees fit to deal with the Indian people, particularly the Sioux tribe in South Dakota. We want a true Indian nation, not one made up of Bureau of Indian Affairs puppets." Tribal chairman Wilson told the press the occupiers were armed with rifles and possibly two machine guns and could "hold out for weeks".

While the occupiers at first had no such plans, Wilson turned out to be right. For ten weeks—from February 27 until May 8—a strange, limited war went on in the windswept South Dakota valley. People were shot at; many were wounded; two were killed. It was a renewed U.S.-Indian war, taking place on the very spot where the last such war had occurred 83 years before. And, as had been the case in 1890, U.S. military strength far outweighed that of the Indians.

Within hours of the seizure of the historic village, about 90 FBI agents and U.S. marshals, members of the Special Operations Group trained to handle domestic crises, surrounded the village. The following day their ranks increased to 250—swollen by federal agents who had been waiting in readiness, billeted in the hotels and motels of nearby towns. It was a turn of events the OSCRO-AIM group had not anticipated. Domestic police agencies—the FBI, the BIA police and the U.S. marshals—were equipped with armed forces personnel carriers (APCs), helicopters, planes, ammunition, high-powered rifles and technical advisors. The APCs, troop-carrying tanks, served as federal bunkers during the siege and became a regular feature on the hills surrounding the village. In all, the 71-day siege of Wounded Knee is estimated to have cost the police forces between five and seven million dollars, including the cost of the equipment supplied covertly and illegally by the Pentagon.

It was not until long after the occupation was over that U.S. journalist Ron Ridenhour disclosed that military operations at Wounded Knee were part of a well-rehearsed government plan—Operation Garden Plot—to quell domestic disturbances. Under the code name Cable Splicer, local police were trained in military counter insurgency techniques to enable them to respond rapidly and efficiently to any civil disturbance. At Wounded Knee the plan was put into action, but the involvement of the armed forces had to be disguised since participation of the military in U.S. domestic affairs is illegal without a presidential order. Thus, while the personnel on the blockades were FBI agents, BIA police and marshals, their training, outfitting and direction was supplied by the Pentagon under the command of the 82nd Airborne Division.

Stated government policy was not to fire until fired upon; yet thousands of rounds were fired into the occupied village before the confrontation ended on May 8. Observers inside the village claimed that in all but one case, the government started firing first. While the 11 hostages at first gave the occupiers some protection against an all-out government attack they were soon released. Some actually chose not to leave the fortified compound that Wounded Knee village had become.

The influx of reporters from all around the country and the world prevented the federal agents from applying the massive force assembled outside the village. As many as 50 reporters a day drove into Wounded Knee under strict government guidelines: no food or liquor could be taken in; gasoline and cigarettes were checked so that none could be left for the occupiers. Government officials insisted that reporters be out of the village by 4:30 p.m. each day. Only government-approved journalists were allowed to enter and no photographs of government positions or agents in them were allowed. Nevertheless, there was considerable sympathy for the occupiers, and demonstrations of support were held in many parts of the country. Food, clothing and medicine were donated and at one point supplies were parachuted into the village.

The occupation was a month old when the government decided to terminate the publicity that it felt was fueling the resistance. On March 26, the village was sealed off to reporters: from that day on, news coverage of the occupation came mainly from government press conferences outside Wounded Knee, ensuring officials a measure of press control. Thus when food and medicine were airlifted to Wounded Knee, the justice department announced that "guns and ammunition have been dropped to the militants". When police arrested "19 college-age males" for possession of "contraband" destined for Wounded Knee they did not mention that the contraband was food. When Frank Clearwater, a North Carolina Indian who had hitch-hiked to South Dakota with his pregnant wife, was killed by government fire the day he arrived, government reports said he was white, not Indian, thus making him an "outside agitator" and his death somehow not as blame-worthy.

This management of the news meant the government no longer had to submit to open scrutiny of its actions. No reporters were on hand to record the heavy firefights or the fact that unarmed stretcher-bearers were fired upon as they carried injured Indians from earthen bunkers to the village field hospital. The handling of the media was an effective aspect of the Garden Plot plan.

Against this well-rehearsed, comprehensive government plan, the Indians had only their .22s, their ingenuity and their spiritual strength. News stories coming out of Wounded Knee focussed on two issues: the violence and the AIM-Wilson factionalism. South Dakota Senator James Abourezk, then chairman of the U.S. Senate Subcommittee on Indian Affairs, noted that "all the press did was to highlight Indians with guns, Indians silhouetted against the sky with more guns".

The heavy gunfire did make it seem to the general public as though Wounded Knee was nothing more than a military occupation resulting from a struggle on one reservation, but for Indians throughout North America it was much more.

The immediate grievances of Pine Ridge and the Oglala Sioux came to stand for Indian grievances everywhere in the United States and in Canada. Wounded Knee, 1973 became a symbol for North American Indian resistance to what they saw as decades of land theft, racism and government paternalism and corruption. It was an uprising against political, cultural and economic domination that had destroyed Indian pride, outlawed Indian religion, kept Indian people poor and hungry and allowed them success only at the expense of giving up all that was Indian. For years those who left the reservations to come to the cities tried to assimilate with white society, passing themselves off as Spanish or Italian when applying for a job. Pressure to conform to the dominant society, fostered by BIA education and relocation policies, filtered back to the reservation where full-blooded Indians gradually took a second-class status beside those who had intermarried and thus were "whiter".

At Wounded Knee, the Indians were saying they'd had enough. From all over North America they came to make their stand, holding out until it seemed as if some of their demands would be met. When, two weeks into the occupation, the government lifted the roadblocks and allowed anyone to leave unconditionally, few did. Instead more people came into the village, including the traditional Sioux chiefs. The Oglalas said they would not leave until their grievances were satisfied. One woman who participated in the occupation expressed her reason for being there this way: "I am a woman who is forced like my great-grandmother, grandmother and mother to see our warriors suffer and get killed. We are tired so we stood up next to our men to stop the injustice and the genocide so long perpetrated by the U.S. government and its policies. As a mother I chose to go to Wounded Knee to make a better tomorrow for my children."

During the ten weeks of the occupation, the village of Wounded Knee became a liberated zone—the independent Oglala Nation—with its own institutions and political structures that made it possible to feed, house and above all, defend those within the blockaded compound. Majority rule was abandoned for consensus decision-making. And Christianity, propagated on Pine Ridge in more than 100 missionary churches, was replaced by a return to traditional Indian spirituality. The once-outlawed religious practices of the Sioux served as a rallying point to unify an otherwise disparate group. No other factor so strengthened the Wounded Knee resistance. Indians smoked the sacred pipe, prayed with the ceremonial peyote and took part in the purifying ceremonies of the sweat lodge. They sought out those who had knowledge about the practices that years before had been forbidden or subjected to the "civilizing" forces of white missionaries.

Nicholas Black Elk, grandson of the famed Sioux medicine man, told the ironic story of his grandfather's baptism, first by Methodist missionaries, then by Catholics and finally by Episcopalians. When the elder Black Elk found out there were 285 organized Christian churches in America, he was shocked. Adding up the years his three conversions had already taken, he decided to return to the earth and his Indian religion.

The elder Black Elk had seen the battlefield remains the day after the massacre at Wounded Knee in 1890 and thought that the "sacred tree of life" died there with chief Big Foot. But he dreamed its roots would one day come to life again, joining all Indian people together.

The younger Black Elk noted that the dozens of tribes represented at the Wounded Knee occupation were joined as one, nourishing the roots and fulfilling the ancient prophecy that tribal unity would come through the Sioux. Spiritual leaders like Black Elk ministered successfully to the wounded with Indian sacred ceremonies, medicines, herbs, peyote and minerals. The occupiers possessed a spiritual purpose and drive that enabled them to hold out against the forces assembled outside the village.

The traditional practices that spiritual leaders like Black Elk and Leonard Crow Dog kept alive were the product of a cultural and political system thousands of years old. They honour the earth, bespeaking a people whose lives depended directly on the sustenance of the earth and who sought to live in harmony with nature, not to subdue or conquer it. The revived practices of Indian spirituality provided the activists with a sense of self-knowledge, a sense of their Indianness, a symbol of Indian pride and a source of action. It was this sense of purpose that prompted warriors to call out from their trenches to the federal agents surrounding them, "Are you ready to die for money?"

The occupiers of Wounded Knee paid a high price for their rebellion. Three Indian people lost their lives during the 71-day siege: an old woman went into a diabetic coma and died; Frank Clearwater, a North Carolina Indian, and Buddy Lamont, an Oglala and a leader of the occupation, were killed by government fire. On the other side, two lawmen were wounded. On May 8 when the occupation ended with a negotiated settlement, it was clear that the Oglala Sioux and the American Indian Movement had won a major battle in their continuing effort to press the United States government for recognition of Indian rights and claims.

Some of the gains produced by the occupation were immediate; others were more ephemeral and harder to gauge. The Pine Ridge Reservation superintendent, long a target of complaints, was transferred to a different BIA post. Tribal chairman Richard Wilson's expenditure records, such as they were, were subjected to an independent audit. The Arapaho tribe in Wyoming recalled for review the long-term land leases held by white ranchers. Early in 1974, the Justice Department responded to a civil rights grievance which might have been ignored but for the attention generated by the occupation.

While the takeover of Wounded Knee put the reservation through a long period of chaos and disorder—property was destroyed, business interrupted, relief cheques delayed and schools closed—reservation residents increasingly came to the conclusion that, as one councillor put it, "Wounded Knee was a boil that had to be lanced."

About a dozen candidates ran for the office of tribal chairman in the primary election the winter following the occupation. AIM leader Russell Means outpolled incumbent Richard Wilson, an outcome widely interpreted as an endorsement by reservation residents of Means' role in the occupation. The AIM leader might have won the general election—which is a run-off between the two highest vote-getters in the primary—had it not been for Wilson's allegedly fraudulent election practices and the refusal of the BIA or the courts to intervene.

The many adverse effects of the occupation on both reservation residents and the American Indian Movement did not become clear until later, however, and on May 8, 1973 there was still a sense that Indian people had triumphed. One woman summed up the results of the action in a poem written on the wall of the Wounded Knee church:

There was a war
All my people came
We held out
As the whole world watched
We won
The drums beat on
We're one.

3/From Shubenacadie to Wounded Knee

The occupation of Wounded Knee brought together people from more than 60 North American tribes: Navahos from New Mexico, Iroquois from New York, Chippewas, Crees, Menominees and many more. These Indians had different languages, histories and cultural practices but they had shared the bitter results of their people's conquest by the more numerous, more powerful European invaders. The problems that precipitated the occupation of Wounded Knee were by no means unique to the Pine Ridge Reservation.

Those who protested at Wounded Knee had all heard stories from their parents and grandparents of land thefts, broken treaties and the corruption of officials supposedly acting in their best interest. They had first-hand experience of racism, paternalism and the effects of Christian schools and missions, which had robbed them of their own tradition and denigrated their heritage, and at the same time denied them a full role in white society. Many had fought their own personal battles with alcoholism, drugs and poverty and were fighting now to assert their rights and to rekindle the pride of their race.

Anna Mae Aquash was among this group, although 2,000 miles and an international boundary separated the Nova Scotia reserves where she was born and raised from the reservations of the plains tribes. She too had grown up in a bleak and poverty-ridden community where unemployment, hunger and poor health were the norm.

The Micmac reserve, five miles outside the village of Shubenacadie, Nova Scotia, is not much larger than a midwestern ranch and its 1,000 acres do not provide a solid economic base for the 600 people who live there. Chronic unemployment is relieved only by a small number of band council jobs. A provincial superhighway passes within a few miles of the reserve, but there is no direct access to the Indian community. A few miles away is the Indian-owned and operated Abenaki Motel, a source of pride to Micmacs, some of whom have made the tables and chairs that furnish its dining room and the objects that decorate it. Handcrafts sold to tourists who flock to the area each summer provide a limited additional income for women like Anna Mae Aquash's sister Rebecca Julian, who has lived in Shubenacadie most of her life.

Housing on the reservation is strung along two dirt roads rutted with potholes. It is almost immediately clear where the reservation begins—where the neat-looking farms and the pavement end. On the reserve are new, cheaply constructed bungalows, some already displaying signs of rapid deterioration. Some of the older two-storey, shingled houses remain near the entrance of the reserve, including the one where Anna Mae lived as a child. There is no landscaping.

The town of Shubenacadie is undergoing something of a boom since the opening of the new Halifax airport. Nova Scotia's capital is only 40 miles to the southeast and the airport is halfway between that city and Shubenacadie. There are still no Indians working in the Shubenacadie supermarket, restaurant or gas station, and Indians don't drink at the Shubenacadie Legion.

When Anna Mae Pictou was born on March 27, 1945, the reservation was even poorer than it is today. Her mother, Mary Ellen Pictou, then 24 years old, was living a hand-to-mouth existence in an effort to support her two children, four-year-old Rebecca and two-year-old Mary. She kept house for friends in return for room and board and did occasional babysitting in return for a package of tobacco and a can of milk. Her third daughter was baptized in the white clapboard Catholic church on the hilltop overlooking the reserve.

Anna Mae's father, Francis Thomas Levi, was a popular fellow, well-known as one of the best fiddlers in the area. His relationship with the headstrong Mary Ellen Pictou was a stormy one, and before Anna Mae was born he left the reserve to work in a logging camp in Maine. Mary Ellen Pictou remained on the reserve, subsisting without income for six months until she finally obtained the meagre welfare payments that became the family's livelihood. For young women with limited education—Mary Ellen Pictou had the equivalent of grade three—there were few choices. The young mother was attractive but outspoken, and liked to have a good time. For the most part, she spent her days with other Shubenacadie women playing cards and gambling. They rose early to finish their chores and then played cards all day, stopping only to feed a crying child or change a diaper.

This rather aimless existence changed abruptly in 1949, when Anna Mae was four years old. Her mother married Noel Sapier, a strict and religious man, whose father and brother were traditional chiefs on the Pictou Landing reserve until the elective council system was introduced there in 1951. Sapier took in Mary Ellen Pictou's three daughters and moved the whole family to Pictou Landing, a 300-acre reserve on the shores of Northumberland Strait.

Today about 35 families live on the Pictou Landing reserve. In the early 1950s it was smaller still, little more than a clearing in the bush by the sea. The beaches were sandy, the clams good, the fish plentiful; but in most other ways the reserve was poverty-stricken. The Sapiers' first house was a weathered shell with inch-wide gaps between the boards that swayed dangerously during severe storms, forcing the family to move outside into the rain. Later they moved into one of several abandoned army houses brought on scows across the bay from the town of Pictou. The wind no longer blew through the walls, but there was still no electricity, running water or central heat. Wood stoves provided warmth and water came from a pump shared by four families; and from an early age the Pictou girls learned to lug water and chop wood. They made do with winter dinners of turnips and potatoes. When a series of miscarriages kept Mary Ellen Sapier hospitalized for long periods, the young sisters assumed all the housekeeping responsibilities.

The family's poverty was not exceptional: few on the reserve were better off and many were poorer. Before his marriage to Mary Ellen Pictou, Noel Sapier had found wartime work in the steel mills of nearby Trenton and New Glasgow, but by the early 1950s he was able to find only the odd temporary job. He earned money carving axe handles and making splints for basketweavers on the reserve. His wife made crepe-paper flowers and baskets of sweetgrass which were sold door-to-door in the nearby towns.

The Sapiers' reputation as strict parents is remembered on the reserve to this day. The children's playground was the area surrounding the house and they were allowed to visit friends only on Sunday. The three girls and their brother Francis, born in 1951, grew up confined to the reserve. There was only one car on the reserve and trips into the nearby towns were infrequent. There was no radio or television, no telephone.

A poor and restricted diet left the children vulnerable to every childhood disease, and with poor transportation and communication they were often left untreated unless an illness became critical. Only good luck saved Anna Mae's young brother Francis; when he swallowed a cup of bleach, the one car on the reserve was available to rush him to the hospital. Anna Mae was always the last to get sick and was considered exceptionally strong and healthy. When she was eight, however, she and her sister Rebecca contracted unusual eye infections, which only later were diagnosed as tuberculosis. By then Anna Mae had also had TB of the lung, but it had cured itself.

As wards of the federal government, reserve families were dependent on the federal Indian agent for all their needs. Clothing, often ill-fitting and inappropriate, was provided by the agent who contracted with an outfitter at the lowest possible cost. The Sapiers received such items as army coats and jodhpurs for the little girls. For the most part Mary Ellen Sapier accepted them, but once, when the clothing the family received was full of moth holes, she drew the line. She and her daughters kept what little was usable and repacked the rest. When the Indian agent came on his regular visit he barely had time to give Anna Mae the customary pat on the head before Mary Ellen hauled out the moth-eaten stuff and confronted him. "Do you think I'm going to dress my kids in these?" she demanded. From then on the agent sent better clothes through a different outfitter. Encouraged by this small victory, Mary Ellen began to send letters to bureaucrats in Halifax and Ottawa after any disputes with the agent. She dictated the letters to her daughter Rebecca, but they were usually to no avail.

A high point of the Sapiers' life was the summer trek to Pine Tree, 30 miles from Pictou Landing, where Noel Sapier worked as a farm hand. Home was a tarpaper teepee set up in a clearing amid tall pine trees near the ocean shore, a spot accessible only by rail. The family cooked over open fires and hauled water from a nearby stream. Later they built a cabin from used barn lumber and brought in a wood stove.

These were free times for the children. Food was more plentiful, since their father brought milk and vegetables from the farm. They played hide-and-seek in the woods, wandered along the shore, swam and fished from makeshift rafts. The isolation drew the family together, and Anna Mae and her sister Mary, in particular, developed a closeness that continued into their adult lives.

Despite her tiny stature, Anna Mae was known as the most daring and determined of the three sisters. One of her riskier exploits was to ride the pig on the farm where Noel Sapier worked. When she mounted, the animal slammed itself broadside against the wall of the barn, again and again. The little girl hung on and got down triumphant, indifferent to the bruises on her legs. Some years later when the children attended school in Pine Tree, they passed daily by several horses in a field meadow. Anna Mae's sport was to get onto the back of one particular white horse and ride until it bucked her to the ground. There were also less dangerous amusements. When the children entertained each other with little shows, Anna Mae excelled at imitations. Her favourite subjects were an old man and woman who visited the family, and when she went into another room, it was hard to distinguish her voice from the voices of the old couple.

Every July 26 the Sapiers and other Maritime Micmacs attended the St. Anne Mission held on the nearby island of Meri-gomish. The three-day holiday included community suppers and sports events, as well as religious ceremonies. It was a time to see friends and relatives from other reserves, a time for prayer and a time to seek cures. During one such mission Anna Mae and Re-becca had their infected eyes washed out with holy water and the cure worked for her older sister, though not for Anna Mae.

Throughout the year the family went to church every Sunday, using Noel Sapier's old prayer books, in which Catholic prayers and masses were translated into Micmac. Ironically, the prayer books were among the last remnants of traditional Micmac cul-ture. Many of the tribe's traditional ceremonies and practices had long been forsaken, and knowledge of the language itself was in-creasingly limited. There was, however, a strong belief in the su-pernatural. In Pictou Landing, one old woman in particular was thought to have especially intense psychic powers. A story often told on the reserve concerns the time a passing train failed to stop for her in the village. Farther down the track the train came to a mysterious halt and was unable to continue its journey until the old woman was assured of a ride and was safely on board.

In the one-room Pictou Landing school where Anna Mae first enrolled, it was not these legends but the mysteries of the Catholic religion that were important. Each child was expected to learn the catechism by memory and to answer theological questions in a few words. Mass and hymn singing often took the place of academic work. Anna Mae's teacher, an ascetic single woman, stressed reli-gion as if all her charges were preparing for a life in the convent or the rectory, and Anna Mae was duly impressed: the only time her mother asked her what she wanted to be her answer was "a nun".

Academic standards were not high and it was easy to get good marks in the reserve school. The atmosphere, despite a plethora of rules and punishments, was not unpleasant. All the children knew each other and shared similar backgrounds and experiences. That changed, however, when the school burned down and Pictou Landing children were bussed to Catholic schools off the reserve. At the age of 11 Anna Mae left this sheltered environment to attend elementary school in nearby New Glasgow. Two years later she entered St. John's Academy in the same town for her junior high school education. By then she was four feet 11 inches tall and weighed 84 pounds—a tiny slip of a girl who was capable of fighting any boy in her class. Throughout her childhood Anna Mae had found it necessary to protect her brother, Francis, six years her junior. He was regarded as a sissy, and in defending him, she had learned how to fight.

On the St. John's registration form Anna Mae listed her hobby as drawing and indicated that she had worked outside the home, leaving unanswered the questions about private music training, dancing and elocution lessons. She began the year strongly with A's in French and spelling, but ended the spring term with failures in all but one subject. There was good reason for her lacklustre performance. Indian children were never particularly welcome in schools off the reserve, though the supporting financial grants from the Department of Indian Affairs were. The schoolyard taunts and racial slurs against lazy drunken Indians were a shocking forewarning of the life awaiting them. And the Indian children were usually blamed for the resulting fights. As she reached adolescence, Anna Mae's response to this conflict was, increasingly, silence and withdrawal. This and her light complexion helped her to escape some of the worst abuse, but she was left in no doubt about her Indianness.

In the same year that the children started school at St. John's, Noel Sapier, whom the Indian agent had been accusing of laziness, died after a long fight with cancer. Their father's death occurred just before Christmas and the Sapier children missed a great deal of school that winter. In the spring their mother took them back to the Shubenacadie reserve. Anna Mae's eldest sister Rebecca, then 17, left home and the reserve to work in Framingham, near Boston, Massachusetts. Life at home changed perceptibly; without Noel Sapier's strict discipline, Anna Mae, Mary and Francis were allowed greater freedom to come and go. Mary Ellen Sapier resumed her gambling. It was not unusual for her to rush home in the evening to pick up a quilt she had made and raffle it off to earn extra money for cigarettes, food and more card-playing.

Some traces of the earlier discipline remained, however. Mary Ellen still enforced a curfew on her daughters, and when Anna Mae wasn't home on time the door was locked. She always found a way to get in, to her mother's apparent surprise and secret satisfaction. Essentially, however, Mary Ellen Sapier made only sporadic efforts to control the children. On one occasion, Anna Mae brought her friend Doris Paul home after a day of visiting and wandering on the reservation roads. They found Mary Ellen sitting at the kitchen table eating a quantity of very fatty pork, her hands and face covered in grease. Anna Mae scolded her, "God, Mom, you shouldn't eat like that. You're right sloppy."

"I like my fat," was her mother's nonchalant reply. Without warning Anna Mae and Doris tackled the older woman and wrestled her to the floor. Taking a handful of the greasy meat, Anna Mae rubbed it all over her mother's face. There was laughter all around, with Mary Ellen joining in good-naturedly and making no attempt to reprimand her daughter.

Away from the familiar surroundings of home and reserve, however, Anna Mae was markedly shy and quiet. When in 1961 at the age of 16 she enrolled in Grade 9 at Milford High School, she was just one more of the faceless Micmac students who didn't achieve academically and didn't participate in extracurricular activities. She shrank from involvement, hanging back when her friends fought the white boys who called them "dosed-up squaws". She seemed to be able to turn a deaf ear to the taunts, but continued to fare badly in her schoolwork. Again, problems at home were interfering with what academic success she might have had. During the winter, her mother suddenly decided to remarry. Without informing anyone but Rebecca—who by then was married and expecting her first child—Mary Ellen packed her bags and left. Mary, Anna Mae and Francis came home from school to find themselves abandoned. Their sister Rebecca, who had returned to the reserve, and her husband Steve Julian, then living on an income of $36 a week, took them in. There was porridge for breakfast and only one other meal. Anna Mae made herself as useful as possible, rising at 2 a.m. and 6 a.m. to feed Rebecca's infant son, showering the baby with attention and affection. The whole desperate situation made it impossible for her to concentrate seriously on school, however, and she dropped out before her examinations.

Faced with the need to support herself in the summer of 1962, Anna Mae joined the family of her friend Doris Paul in the annual mass migration of Maritime Indians to Maine. The reserves became ghost towns as the able-bodied boarded up the windows of their homes, packed old cars and headed south to seek work as farm labourers. This was not an entirely new experience for Anna Mae. When she was 11 her mother had taken all the children to the blueberry fields and the tarpaper camps of the migrant workers despite the objections of Noel Sapier. Anna Mae was familiar with the hard work, the beds of straw, the lack of running water and the absence of sanitary facilities of any kind. Blueberry pickers could set their own pace, and many worked a 15-hour day. Teenagers like Anna Mae and Doris Paul, however, usually worked just enough to cover their room, board, clothes and entertainment. The hot July and August afternoons were perfect for swimming and for meeting boys from other reserves.

That year, for the first time, Anna Mae stayed on for the September and October potato harvest, an altogether different and more gruelling kind of work. The days were short and the nights, cold. The pace of work was determined by the need to pick clean before nightfall all the fields dug by tractor to prevent overnight frost damage to the crop. This was dawn-to-dusk, backbreaking work with no time for idling. Those who worked hard throughout the blueberry and potato season cleared about $1,000, while others like Anna Mae earned much less.

The harvest over, Anna Mae sent word to Rebecca that she was not coming back to the reserve but was going to Boston. As she was about to leave the farm, the boy she had been going out with began to fight with another boy over the privilege of taking her to the city. When they finally asked Anna Mae herself which one she wanted to go with she replied, "Neither one of you." Pointing to Jake Maloney who was watching from the sidelines, she said, "I want to go with him."

Jake Maloney, a Micmac from Shubenacadie, was a short,

broad-shouldered, handsome young man who seemed to want to make something of himself. He and Anna Mae became part of the steady stream of Micmacs who each year migrated to Boston in search of work and a better future. They were more fortunate than many of these Indians who soon found themselves on skid row, homeless, jobless, friendless and drunk.

In Boston, Anna Mae first stayed with a Micmac friend who had come to the city several years earlier and who freely opened her South Boston apartment to newcomers. Some nights the apartment floor was wall-to-wall beds. Anna Mae soon found a job as a packer in a factory and quickly began to learn city ways and new social skills. Her friends remember that she learned how to dance listening to scratchy records on a borrowed portable record player. On her days off she wandered around the city, gazing into department store windows, dreaming of things she would one day own, struck by the differences between life on the reserve and that of the majority of white Bostonians.

The Micmac newcomers were often dazzled by the attractions of the city and the new, seemingly endless possibilities it offered. At first they welcomed the anonymity of city life. In Boston the non-white minorities did not stand out the way they did in the smaller Canadian cities—Halifax for example. At the same time the size, demands and unfamiliarity of the city left the Indians feeling confused and often lonely. As a group they found themselves caught between the white and black communities, belonging to neither and looked down on by both.

In June 1964, Anna Mae, then 19, gave birth to her first child by Jake Maloney, a daughter Denise. She was living on welfare and sharing an apartment with her sister Mary, who gave birth to triplets at about the same time. The sisters, always close as children, reared their babies together. Mary, the more serious of the two, was more likely to feel intimidated by the strange and difficult new circumstances. Anna Mae's style, whatever she felt, was to face the unknown with a show of bravado.

The following summer, Anna Mae, pregnant with Jake Maloney's second child, went to Indian Island, New Brunswick to stay with her mother and Mary Ellen's third husband, Wilfred Barlow.

His brother, chief of the tiny reservation, became Anna Mae's tutor in Micmac history. She plied him with questions about Micmac tradition and ceremonies and borrowed books from him on the subject. In September, shortly after their second daughter Deborah was born, Anna Mae and Jake were married in Richibucto, New Brunswick, not far from the Indian Island Reserve where Anna Mae's mother lived. After the traditional Catholic ceremony the young couple drove 250 miles south to Shubenacadie for a wedding party and then returned to Boston.

Jake Maloney had been working as a janitor at the Ritz Hotel, but he regarded it as a dead-end job from which he had to escape. He began taking karate lessons twice a week at George Matson's studio in Boston, encouraged by his wife who shared his desire for self-improvement. Anna Mae became his sparring partner and became proficient in the martial art, though she took no formal lessons herself.

In the fall of 1966, when her younger daughter was just a year old, Anna Mae began work at Elvin Selow, a small family-owned sewing factory, stitching boat cushions and toboggan pads at piece rates. Her earnings ranged from $30 to $100 weekly. She stayed with the job for two years and was promoted to a job closing cushions at a combination of piece-work rates and hourly wage. When she left at the end of 1968, Anna Mae was considered by the management to be one of the most reliable and productive workers. She recommended Indian friends in need of jobs to her employer and helped a number of Micmacs obtain work.

The young couple settled into a fairly comfortable life in Boston. They put money into the bank and gradually outfitted their apartment with modern appliances and furniture which Anna Mae described with pride in letters home to her family. Anna Mae also took pride in Jake's steady progress at the karate school. In her spare time she taught herself to type and play the guitar, and diligently went through the child psychology book she had borrowed from her sister, underlining important passages. She and Jake showed deep concern for the way their children were raised. Denise and Deborah were more carefully disciplined than children in other Micmac families; friends noted that the girls were expected to eat all the food on their plates and were sent to bed at specific times. At the same time the young mother took time to explain to them the reason for certain rules. She spent long hours playing with and singing to them and took them with her whenever possible.

While in many respects Anna Mae was better off than she had ever been, she had strong doubts about the white, urban lifestyle she was moving into. She often told friends that before her daughters reached school age the family would go back home. She wanted her children educated as Indians, not in the tough urban ghetto schools. Part of Anna Mae's concern arose from the plight of other Micmacs in Boston. She became increasingly intent on doing something for her people, particularly the youngsters who dropped out of school without skills and without a future. She tried to help one young boy who was consistently in trouble by getting him a job at the Selow sewing factory and urging him to settle down. These larger concerns about the fate of other Indian people were expressed more and more often.

For his part Jake Maloney was finding a career in karate. George Matson first helped him find a better-paying job and then, convinced of his student's aptitude, invited him to invest in the karate school and learn about its organization and operation. Jake was eager, but Anna Mae was not. The $1,000 required represented the sum total of their savings. In 1968, despite Anna Mae's objections, Jake made the investment and began serving his apprenticeship at the school were he soon became known as "Mr. Karate". Further tensions arose between Jake and Anna Mae as a result of his involvement with the karate studio. Early in 1969 his barely concealed love affair with a young white woman at the school came out into the open, a discovery that hurt his wife deeply. Anna Mae loved and respected Jake and had devoted herself to him and their two daughters. Now she felt completely betrayed. She left Jake and her job at Elvin Selow, taking her children with her. Three months later they were reconciled but it soon became clear that the marriage would not work. For the most part, Anna Mae refused to discuss her marital problems, confiding only in one or two close friends. To others, she would say, "There's no point in being sad. If they don't want you, there's no use in hanging on."

With the break-up of the marriage, Anna Mae's lifestyle changed considerably. She began to spend more time in the "combat zone"—Boston's strip of cheap bars and flophouses—and cultivated friends whose lives revolved around alcohol and bars. An incident from this period shows how she was changing. Anna Mae and her sister Mary were part of a large group of Indians drinking in Kelly's bar when a fight broke out between a white man and one of their group—a huge woman nicknamed Savage. Savage was stabbed in the stomach, but when the police came they arrested the victim and not her assailant. Anna Mae was furious. Outside the bar, where a group had gathered to watch the proceedings, she began shouting at the police officers, telling them that it was the man who should be taken away; then she began to fight with her friend's assailant. The police broke up the fight, shoving both of them into the paddy wagon. More scuffling broke out inside and as the officers attempted to stop it, Anna Mae climbed onto the roof of the police vehicle and then jumped onto the officers, knocking them to the sidewalk. She was jailed overnight as a result of the incident, but was released the next morning with a small fine.

During this period, however, Anna Mae usually found more constructive outlets. In the summer of 1969, Philip Young, a young Micmac artist from New Brunswick hitch-hiking to Woodstock for the famed festival, found himself instead in the combat zone, drunk. He and others subsequently began a small group therapy program for Indian alcoholics. The Boston Indian Council (BIC) evolved from these meetings, and Anna Mae was among the early organizers. From a modest third-floor office at 155 Tremont Avenue, the council's activities grew to include drug and alcohol education, a job placement program, a housing service and after-school programs for Indian children. The council office became a friendship centre and meeting place.

Almost from the beginning there was a struggle for control of the council between Micmacs, other Indian groups and individuals claiming to be Indian. Misuse of grants by the non-Indian executive director resulted in a demonstration and picket against him. Anna Mae was active in the campaign, which successfully ousted the controversial administration. She also acted as a volunteer community worker, visiting Indian homes to discuss problems and making regular reports to the BIC executive.

The Boston Indian Council suffered from the usual rivalry between moderates and militants as it faced the perennial dilemma of most self-help organizations. To be effective, the organization must demand substantial reforms, but militant actions to promote the needed changes would risk its government funding. Despite this problem, members of the council helped plan and took part in the demonstration at the *Mayflower II* on Thanksgiving Day 1970, a symbolic protest against the arrival of Europeans in North America. Russell Means and other members of the American Indian Movement were involved in the demonstration and thus the link was made between AIM and east coast Indian people.

That fall Anna Mae left the Elvin Selow factory to teach at TRIBE (Teaching and Research in Bicultural Education), an Indian learning and cultural centre near Bar Harbor, Maine. The project, created by a group of Penobscot, Passamaquoddy and Micmac Indians, was located on an evacuated Job Corps site in Acadia National Park and was funded by both American and Canadian governments and private foundations. Its aim was to show that Indian students who had dropped out of school could learn successfully in a setting that allowed them to feel pride in their own culture and heritage. Anna Mae was one of ten staff members who taught academic subjects in addition to arts, crafts, music and dancing. With junior and high-school age students, she reviewed standard textbooks, discussing and challenging their distortions of the historical role attributed to Indians.

For Anna Mae TRIBE was a dream come true. Denise and Deborah were with her and became part of her work as she and other instructors explored ways to instil pride and motivation in the Indian youth. Anna Mae gained a reputation as a person in a hurry for change, while some of her colleagues were more content with the prospect of gradual gains. To some it seemed she was still searching for the best way to apply her energies, but at the same time she was happier and more carefree than she had been for months.

Erratic funding resulted in a complete turnover of TRIBE staff in the spring of 1971. The project received further grants the following year and then was terminated. Those involved in the school did not believe, as did the funding agencies, that the program was a failure. For individuals like Anna Mae, it had been a rich learning experience. She had revived and expanded her knowledge of Micmac, increased her understanding of history as it affected Indian people, and learned some of the basics of teaching methods, school organization and administration.

In September 1971, Anna Mae, at the age of 26, enrolled in a New Careers program at Boston's Wheelock College. In a course designed for mature students, she combined academic studies with practical work as a teaching assistant in the Ruggles Street Day Care Centre in Roxbury, a low income, predominantly black area of Boston. The day care centre was housed in a church auditorium, its two classrooms separated by makeshift dividers which did little to muffle the sounds of 40 to 50 preschoolers. Despite these difficult accommodations, which made heavy demands on all the staff, Anna Mae was a success. None of her co-workers remembered her ever losing patience with the children. Instead she impressed her co-workers with her strength, energy, imagination and reliability. She brought Indian costumes, artifacts and pictures; baked bannock and taught Indian history; and wrote songs which she taught to the youngsters.

Ruggles Street Day Care soon became a place where the problems, hopes and aspirations of Indian people were vividly portrayed. According to co-worker Sally Davis, Anna Mae was offered a scholarship to the prestigious Brandeis University following her success at Wheelock. It must have been a triumphant moment for the former grade nine dropout whose teachers had long ago dismissed her—and other Indian children like her—as poor academic material. But Anna Mae did not accept the offer. Her decision was influenced by her personal problems; the need to care for and support her daughters; the perennial shortage of money; and most important, an increased commitment to Indian struggles. Instead of becoming a Brandeis student, she became more involved in community work in the Dorchester ghetto.

With Nogeeshik Aquash, a Chippewa artist from Ontario who had by then become her lover, she helped establish a job placement program for Indians in the Boston area. Urging affirmative action in the hiring of minorities, the pair were successful in obtaining jobs for a number of Indian people at the General Motors plant in Framingham, near Boston. Anna Mae herself worked on the assembly line for several weeks. For Indian people, used to the backbreaking work of the blueberry and potato farms and dead-end city jobs at low pay, the assembly line work was comparatively easy and financially rewarding. Wages of close to $6 an hour for jobs involving dexterity and concentration rather than intense physical labour meant that the Indians found it difficult to sympathize with the grievances of plant workers.

In November 1972, Anna Mae and others from the Boston Indian Council joined the occupation of the Bureau of Indian Affairs building in Washington which climaxed AIM's Trail of Broken Treaties caravan. The Boston contingent remained for only a short time but made it clear that they supported the protests of the Indian activists assembled from all over the United States and Canada.

The 27-year-old woman who participated in that demonstration was not the same Anna Mae who married Jake Maloney. She had abandoned the bleached beehive hairdo which had once symbolized her attempt to become a proper young matron and generally devoted less attention to her personal appearance. She was thinner, wore her hair long and loose, dressed in blue jeans and often went barefoot. The fun-loving Anna Mae was now more serious and earnest, particularly when she was with her children.

Her new lover, Nogeeshik Aquash, was a flamboyant and elegant man who emphasized his Indian pride by a striking use of costume, jewellery and beadwork. He was in part responsible for the scepticism which Anna Mae's friends and family in Nova Scotia felt about what was clearly a new direction in her life. On first meeting Nogeeshik, her mother exclaimed with characteristic bluntness, "My God, Annie Mae! Where'd you get the last of the

Mohicans?'' Others were equally astonished by Aquash's style and unconventional sense of humour and dubbed him "a crazy Indian". The exception was Rebecca Julian, who noted approvingly that Anna Mae had more personal freedom with Nogeeshik than in her marriage to Jake Maloney.

The relationship was not without its problems, however. The fine edge of Aquash's idealism was often blunted by alcohol and at such times he taunted Anna Mae with his shortcomings. Her usual repsonse was to ignore him, but only to a point. Anna Mae's sister Mary and her husband Earl Lafford witnessed one such exchange which led to a bitter argument. Listening from the kitchen they became alarmed at the ferocity of the fight in the living room, and when the two came to blows, Earl sent Mary to investigate. She returned grinning. "Don't worry. She's taking care of herself."

When the occupation of Wounded Knee took place in the spring of 1973, Anna Mae and Nogeeshik decided, despite the obvious danger, to cast their lot with the protesters. Anna Mae had not stopped believing in the need for systematic community work, but at the same time she began to see the need for a more dramatic show of protest, for quicker, more noticeable results. Wounded Knee was the place to show solidarity and bear witness. The most difficult obstacle to the journey was the care of Deborah and Denise, and after much deliberation, Anna Mae decided to leave the children with her sister Mary. Then, dressed fashionably to avoid the suspicion which would fall on any radical-looking Indian going to South Dakota, she set out for Wounded Knee, claiming to be a legal secretary.

In preparation for the final leg of the trip into the besieged South Dakota village, Anna Mae and Nogeeshik Aquash camped at Crow Dog's Paradise on the Rosebud Reservation, 90 miles east of Pine Ridge village. Henry Crow Dog and his son Leonard, the AIM spiritual leader, had agreed to let their land be used as a staging area for the food, medical supplies and arms which outside supporters collected and attempted to smuggle into Wounded Knee. On the appointed day Anna Mae and others left Rosebud in two vans. The first vehicle, containing most of the group's supplies and guns was stopped; the second, carrying Anna Mae and Nogeeshik, escaped detection and made its way over the backroads to a drop-off point about eight miles from Wounded Knee. At dusk, the couple and several food runners began the overland hike through the hills and rolling gulchland into the compound. Heavy government patrols prevented their passage and they were forced to stay hidden for the long day that followed. When it was dark again they crept through the patrol lines and entered the village, exhausted and hungry but jubilant.

In the days that followed, Anna Mae emerged as a cool head and hard worker among the occupiers of Wounded Knee. During the heavy volleys of government gunfire that riddled the village and the makeshift accommodations of the occupiers, Anna Mae impressed others with her ability to keep calm and retain a sense of humour. During one particularly heavy exchange of gunfire while thousands of rounds of ammunition were shot into the village, Anna Mae and other women rolled cigarettes for the warriors outside. They calmly discussed their personal histories and how they had begun to take part in Indian struggles in a way that helped allay fear and distract everyone's thinking from the possibility of death. Anna Mae helped dig bunkers and was one of the few women who took part in the nightly patrols of the village. She considered herself a female warrior and did not hesitate to take on work usually done by the men.

Anna Mae and Nogeeshik seemed more impressed and inspired than many by what was happening at Wounded Knee. In mid-April, within days of their arrival, the couple were married in a traditional Sioux ceremony. The event symbolized their return to traditional values and served to emphasize the important role of Indian spiritualism in creating unity among the protesters. The wedding occurred one day after a young Sioux woman had given birth and, like the advent of a new life, was a sign of commitment and a prayer for unity and renewal in the Independent Oglala Nation.

The Wounded Knee trading post was hardly large enough to accommodate all the well-wishers and onlookers. Anna Mae was dressed in a dark cape and blue jeans, her hair tied with a red ribbon. Nogeeshik, a British .303 rifle slung over his shoulder, strutted in brown corduroy trousers trimmed with fur and a black felt hat which sported an eagle feather. Whenever Anna Mae teased him, his back straightened and he thrust out his chest to display the beaded owl which hung from a long black scarf around his neck. During the wedding, gifts were exchanged, promises made, the peace pipe passed. Ninety flesh offerings were cut from the arms of the couple's eight attendants for the bride and to hon-our Mother Earth. Spiritual leader Nicholas Black Elk performed the ceremony and told the couple he had only the power to unite: "The Great Spirit did not give me the power for divorce. You are always together now." For Anna Mae the wedding bespoke her determination to live a truly Indian way of life. Her participation at Wounded Knee marked her as a person dedicated to Indian struggles and established her as an AIM sympathizer and sup-porter.

Anna Mae Aquash's increasing personal involvement with and commitment to AIM coincided with the most difficult stages of the movement's growing conflict with the United States govern-ment. AIM's moral victory at Wounded Knee embarrassed the government and more than ever marked the organization as a rallying point for the growing dissent among North American In-dians who demanded social justice, collective rights and the oppor-tunity to live in dignity in their own land. The success at Wounded Knee made AIM a target for attack, particularly by the FBI, which in the wake of Wounded Knee increased its efforts to disrupt AIM, discredit its leaders and strike fear into its supporters. Like other civil rights organizations that fought vigorously for equality and justice, AIM became a prime target for the United States sec-ret police.

Anna Mae and Nogeeshik Aquash left Wounded Knee before the occupation ended on May 8, 1973, after spending about a month in the occupied village. They faced only minor charges of violating reservation law for their participation in the incident, but in the months that followed pressures intensified for those who continued the fight for Indian rights. The risks had seemed great when high-powered bullets ripped through the flimsy shelters of

Wounded Knee village; they became even greater when the occupation ended and the battle became a covert one, no longer open to public scrutiny and unrestrained by public opinion. From the comparative safety of community organizing in Boston, Anna Mae Aquash entered a far deadlier political environment as a result of her participation at Wounded Knee.

4/The FBI's Secret War on Dissent

From the time of the American Revolution, the United States has prided itself on its traditions of freedom of speech, association and religious belief, and has affirmed these virtues as the standards by which other nations should be judged. In recent years, however, repeated revelations of secret police activities designed to stifle organized dissent and to discredit dissenters have undermined this democratic image.

Internationally, the Central Intelligence Agency has been deeply embroiled in the internal affairs of foreign countries, plotting the overthrow of governments and the assassination of political leaders. The CIA overstepped its legal mandate by conducting spy and counterintelligence operations at home, and in doing so competed with the FBI, the agency officially responsible for U.S. domestic security. The FBI itself has operated with similar disregard for the law: for years it illegally tapped telephones, intercepted mail and compiled dossiers on tens of thousands of American citizens it deemed threatening or potentially threatening to American national security. The result was that organizations struggling to achieve social change faced secret police agencies which equated dissent with subversion and political action with treason and which fought dissent on a scale, and with a dedication, that threatened the very foundations of American democracy.

By the mid-1970s, there was considerable public concern about the role of U.S. intelligence agencies, both at home and abroad. Responding to this concern, the United States Senate appointed a

Select Committee to Study Governmental Operations with Respect to Intelligence Activities. Chaired by Democratic Senator Frank Church, this group is commonly known as the Select Committee on Intelligence or the Church committee. In January 1975, it began a lengthy inquiry into the activities of both the CIA and the FBI. The investigation made public further information about the illegal and unconstitutional programs and activities of America's political police, confirming many of the public's worst fears about the extent of their autonomy and the extremity of their actions. At first it was thought that the FBI and the CIA had escaped the control of both Congress and the President, but it soon became clear that highly placed elected officials had approved and encouraged much of the illegal activity.

The Church committee investigated the FBI's operations against groups which had been identified by the Bureau as dangerous to the state. These included Martin Luther King Jr.'s Southern Christian Leadership Conference, a small U.S. leftist political party, the Socialist Workers Party, and the militant Black Panther Party. The Church investigations stopped before they reached the FBI's operation dealing with the American Indian Movement and other Indian organizations, but the information revealed in the three other cases gives a clear picture of the political modus operandi used by the FBI in dealing with groups like AIM.

The seemingly new problem of illegal police activity is in fact not new at all, but reaches back to the early twentieth-century origins of the FBI. From its very beginnings the FBI was a political as well as a conventional police force, an extension of the Bureau of Investigation created by President Theodore Roosevelt in 1908. It was while working for this organization that the young J. Edgar Hoover first began keeping index cards on several hundred political radicals. By the time Hoover died in 1972, after nearly 50 years as chief federal lawman, the handful of index cards had turned into millions of computerized files. Targets of FBI investigations included pacifists, civil rights activists, members of Congress and news reporters. Bureau abuses went largely unnoticed by white middle-class Americans until the Vietnam war. During that period, many law-abiding citizens were surprised to find that democratic dissent from U.S. foreign policy was an open invitation for investigation by FBI agents.

During the First World War, J. Edgar Hoover headed the General Intelligence Division, which conducted investigations of "potential enemy aliens". He developed a list of persons to be detained in the event of a national emergency, which the government used to arrest 6,000 resident aliens, detaining over 2,000 in violation of their constitutional rights. In 1918, the Bureau arrested without warrants more than 50,000 men suspected of draft evasion. In the 1920s the agency developed information on alleged anarchists, communists, labour organizers and political dissidents, enabling Attorney General A. Mitchell Palmer to authorize an infamous series of nation-wide raids that resulted in the arrest of 10,000 persons who were detained and denied bail but never brought to trial.

In 1924, J. Edgar Hoover became director of the scandal-ridden FBI and began immediately to refurbish the agency's image. He created the popular image of honest, alert and invincible "G-men" relentless in their opposition to gangsters and crime. He also invented the Public Enemy List of the 1930s which focussed on the FBI's pursuit of colourful small-time outlaws like John Dillinger, Pretty Boy Floyd and Machine Gun Kelly. Public praise of the Bureau rose to great heights, obscuring the agency's political role. By the 1960s Hoover had become so powerful a political and cultural influence that he personally was able to control the lead casting in the weekly television series, "The FBI", which perpetuated the Bureau's crime-busting image. Hoover's files on political figures were so extensive that while various U.S. presidents harboured doubts about the extent of his power, none dared challenge his authority openly. Hoover had become untouchable and retained his position until his death in 1972, well beyond the normal retirement age.

Under Hoover, the FBI conducted a limited investigation of Nazism and fascism in the United States in the 1930s, but its energies were concentrated on the communist movement. During the Second World War, President Franklin D. Roosevelt authorized the FBI to investigate espionage and sabotage within the

United States, and under this mandate the agency increased its investigation of "communist influence" in many American organizations. In 1947 Congress established the Central Intelligence Agency as the international counterpart of the FBI, and the two organizations cooperated closely during the Cold War years.

When Congress adopted the loyalty program in 1950, it gave the FBI exclusive jurisdiction to conduct "name checks" and full background investigations to determine which organizations should be placed on the Attorney General's list. The FBI also developed a "Security Index" naming individuals to be arrested in the event of a national emergency. The House Committee on Unamerican Activities (HUAC) investigation into breaches of government security, the trial and imprisonment of Alger Hiss, the Rosenberg spy case and the widespread communist witch hunt led by Senator Joseph McCarthy all increased public apprehension about subversives. The Bureau took advantage of the Cold War climate of fear and suspicion to expand further its jurisdiction, budget and activities.

By 1955, according to the Annual Report of the U.S. Attorney General, the FBI was monitoring the "entire spectrum of the social and labor movement in the country". By the most generous estimates of the Bureau itself, membership in the Communist Party never exceeded 80,000, yet the FBI opened 432,000 files on "subversive" Americans during the 1950s. An estimated 5,000 "subversive informants" were employed to infiltrate organizations and collect information. In the following decade both the number of files and the number of informants tripled.

The concern of the Church committee in 1975-76 was to determine to what extent the FBI had exceeded its mandate to keep watch on subversives and had engaged actively in counterintelligence work by fomenting discord, spreading misinformation, encouraging illegal activity and in various other ways disrupting and discrediting organizations which it viewed unfavourably. The committee report, made public on April 28, 1976, revealed that the FBI was indeed heavily involved in counterintelligence operations directed against various organizations. Some, like the Black Panther Party and the Socialist Workers Party, never gained substantial public support. The Bureau, however, did not limit its activities to fringe organizations of the left and minority groups. It looked upon the entire civil rights movement as a threat to U.S. national security, as was made clear by its unscrupulous campaign against the non-violent Southern Christian Leadership Conference and its leader, Martin Luther King Jr.

The modern black civil rights movement in the United States began to gain momentum late in 1955 after a black woman, Rosa Parks, was arrested in Montgomery, Alabama for refusing an order to move to the back of a city bus. Mrs. Parks' arrest touched off a 382-day transit boycott by Montgomery blacks intent on ending segregated seating and ushered in more than a decade of protest and non-violent confrontation to end long-established patterns of racial segregation. Freedom rides, sit-ins, boycotts, marches and candlelight vigils followed the successful bus boycott and brought to prominence and international acclaim the young southern minister, Martin Luther King, Jr.

King attracted the attention of the FBI in mid-1957 by giving a speech on the evils of racial prejudice to demonstrators attending a "Prayer Pilgrimage" in Washington, D.C. King promised that his organization, the Southern Christian Leadership Conference (SCLC) would organize a voter registration drive for southern blacks. In Hoover's view that was enough to make King a potentially dangerous subversive, and for the FBI to begin covert surveillance under its classification, "racial matters". Hoover told his G-men in a memo, "In view of the stated purpose of the organization, you should remain alert...." For agents this order meant that King and those who followed him would be fair game for intensive investigation, harassment and, in many cases, outright physical assault.

In their insatiable search for subversives, FBI agents carefully confined their investigation to the potential for crime within the SCLC and among King's associates in the civil rights movement. Assaults and other crimes committed against civil rights workers by their opponents went largely uninvestigated and unprosecuted. Marchers and demonstrators in the late 1950s and early 1960s

were repeatedly subjected to beatings, firehosings, attacks by police dogs, death threats and other abuses. Whenever it could, the
FBI looked the other way; and when it could not, perfunctory
investigations almost invariably failed to produce results, despite
the Bureau's vaunted reputation as an efficient upholder of the
law.

By mid-1962, King had begun to capture the imagination not
only of black Americans, but of a sizeable number of white sympathizers both at home and abroad. Continually harassed and
arrested in southern towns on such minor charges as parading
without a permit, King increasingly became the focus of intense
media coverage. In response, Hoover stepped up his campaign to
discredit King. No longer satisfied to collect information, Hoover
took the offensive. He ordered a review of Bureau files to *prepare*
"subversive" information on King "suitable for dissemination"
to FBI allies in the press and elsewhere. King was by then listed as
a communist and was designated as one of the many persons to be
rounded up and jailed in the event of a national emergency.

The FBI's real onslaught against King began, however, following the young minister's response to the Bureau's early smear
campaign. King vehemently denied the managed press reports,
generally attributed to "reliable sources" in the U.S. Department
of Justice, which suggested that he and his colleagues maintained
affiliations with communists. King countered by criticizing the FBI
for selective non-enforcement of the law and cited indisputable
evidence that its agents had stood idly by while local citizens,
sheriffs and their deputies violated the constitutional rights of
southern blacks whose only offense had been participation in
peaceful demonstrations. He spoke of his people's distrust of the
FBI and noted that most of its agents in the South were white
southerners who shared the racial prejudices of the community at
large. "To maintain their status," King said, "they have to be
friendly with the local police and with people who are promoting
segregation."

Hoover was infuriated by King's accusations. Former assistant
FBI director William Sullivan recently told the Church committee
that King's public criticism of the FBI made Hoover "very

upset....I think behind it all was the racial bias, the dislike of Negroes, the dislike of the civil rights movement....I do not think he could rise above that." Hoover told Sullivan he would never have a black in the FBI as long as he was director. King had pinpointed what Sullivan called Hoover's "cozy relationship" with southern sheriffs. "They helped us on bank robberies and such, and they kept the black man in his place. Hoover didn't want anything to upset that relationship with law enforcement authorities in the South."

In August 1963, 250,000 marchers, organized by a variety of U.S. groups, demonstrated in Washington, D.C. in support of pending civil rights legislation. They, and listeners around the world, heard King's famous "I Have a Dream" speech as an eloquent plea for racial harmony and justice. But internal FBI reports characterized the speaker as "demagogic": "We must mark him now...as the most dangerous Negro of the future of this nation from the standpoint of Communism, the Negro and national security."

In order to accomplish this, the FBI moved into high gear. Unable to link him to communism, the Bureau switched to character assassination and Hoover circulated diatribes against King among Washington officials. Illegal wiretaps and secret microphones were installed in King's hotel rooms on 16 known occasions. Andrew Young, now U.S. ambassador to the United Nations and an aide to King at the time, reported that a bug was even found in the pulpit of a church in Selma, Alabama in 1965.

All this resulted from top-level FBI plans to use every possible "investigative technique" to discredit King. Evidence gathered by the Church committee shows that FBI strategists proposed to employ "disgruntled" acquaintances, ministers, "colored" agents, "aggressive" newsmen, King's housekeeper and even his wife in the attempts to obtain information which could be used to disgrace him. One written proposal suggested "placing a good-looking female plant in King's office". The FBI desperately wanted evidence of extra-marital and preferably inter-racial sexual activities. Such information, if made public, would impair the minister's moral authority and thereby diminish his political appeal.

King was neither the first nor the last target of the Bureau's illegal bugs and wiretaps designed to spy on personal lives for purposes of political blackmail. Presidents and congressmen alike feared J. Edgar Hoover because they knew of his private collection of information on prominent individuals. Hoover's unassailable power stemmed in part from his astute use of these skeletons-in-the-closet to control rivals and critics.

Despite the FBI's smear campaign, Martin Luther King became an honoured and acclaimed public figure. When he was chosen by *Time* as 1963 Man of the Year, Hoover scribbled across a memo, "They had to dig deep in the garbage to come up with this one." When King was scheduled to meet with Pope Paul VI, Hoover tried to intervene. The audience took place anyway and Hoover's notation on a related memo read "Astounding".

Whenever it could, the FBI tried to subvert ceremonies to honour King, while agents whispered seamy sex stories to journalists who would listen. The Bureau offered taped information allegedly obtained from clandestine hotel bugs to newspapers and magazines. It arranged for the Internal Revenue Service to conduct a harassing audit of the SCLC and tried to prevent foundation and church funds from being channelled into the civil rights movement. The FBI attempted to dissuade magazine and book publishers from printing material favourable to King, and it continued to leak false information about him and the organizations he represented.

One of the FBI's most reprehensible acts occurred in 1964, only 34 days before King was to receive the Nobel Peace Prize. The Bureau mailed King copies of tapes allegedly recorded in his Washington, D.C. hotel room. A covering letter urged King to commit suicide or face revelation of the information on the tapes. The letter read in part:

> King, look into your heart. There is only one thing left. You know what it is. You have just 34 days in which to do it (this exact number has been selected for a specific reason, it has definite practical significance). You are done. Your "honorary" degrees, your Nobel Prize, (what a grim farce) and other awards will not save you. King, I repeat, you are

done. There is but one way out for you. You better take it before your filthy fraudulent self is bared to the nation.

The Church committee concluded its report on the FBI's campaign against Martin Luther King in this way: "The actions taken against Dr. King are indefensible. They represent a sad episode in the dark history of covert actions directed against law-abiding citizens by a law enforcement agency."

The "episode" may not yet be closed, for considerable suspicion still surrounds FBI activities at the time of the civil rights leader's assassination. A curious FBI "blind memo" approved by FBI Director Hoover himself, and recently made public, was designed to "publicize [King's] hypocrisy". The March 28, 1968 memo, intended for distribution to "cooperative news media", states: "The fine Hotel Lorraine in Memphis is owned and patronized exclusively by Negroes, but King did not go there," staying instead at a "plush Holiday Inn Motel, white-owned, operated and almost exclusively white patronized."

When King returned to Memphis he changed hotel rooms apparently in response to criticism stemming from the news release. He was murdered on April 4, 1968 while standing outside his room at the Hotel Lorraine. James Earl Ray, an escaped petty criminal who pleaded guilty to the killing, has since denied killing King and claims he was an unwitting dupe in an assassination plot. The U.S. House of Representatives Assassinations Committee is still studying innumerable bits of evidence in the case, including allegations by a 27-year veteran of the Louisville, Kentucky police force that $500,000 was offered for King's assassination in a plot involving Louisville police officers and FBI agents. The committee continues to investigate the possibility of a conspiracy in King's death.

In the campaign against Martin Luther King, the FBI used only some of the diverse and extreme measures that have become standard in its counterintelligence work against dissenting political groups. Still others were revealed as a result of the Church committee's investigation of activities against the Socialist Workers Party and the better-known Black Panther Party as well as through lawsuits launched against the Bureau by both groups. They provide still further insight into the methods and tactics used by the FBI and into the mentality prevailing in the Bureau immediately before and during the time it launched its attacks on the American Indian Movement.

On March 29, 1976, evidence submitted in a $37 million civil damage suit by the Socialist Workers Party against the FBI revealed that specially-trained teams of FBI agents had routinely and illegally burglarized the party's offices between 1960 and 1966. In response to federal court orders, the FBI turned over documents showing it had committed 94 burglaries, an average of one every three weeks, for six and a half years. Agents stole and photographed thousands of documents, including personal correspondence, names of campaign contributors and the legal defence strategies of party members in pending court cases. The stolen information was used by the FBI to disrupt the SWP's legal political activities. The Bureau, the Church committee noted, "has conceded that the SWP has never been engaged in organizational violence". Additional court orders have disclosed that more than 1,300 informers were used from 1960 to 1976 to penetrate the small party, whose membership never exceeded 2,500. More than $1.6 million in cash was paid to 301 of these; the FBI has provided no information on the amounts paid to the remaining 1,000.

According to legal briefs submitted in the lawsuit, 42 of the informers actually held office within the SWP and the Young Socialist Alliance and two ran for elected public office in the name of the party. During its 38-year investigation of the SWP the only federal criminal charges brought against party members as a result of party activities were the indictment of 18 leaders in 1940 on charges of violating sections of the anti-subversive Smith Act which were later ruled unconstitutional.

Documents released to the SWP show that since 1960 the FBI has maintained an army of some 1,300 free-floating informers to spy on the members and activities of a wide range of groups including the SWP. This tallies roughly with a congressional committee estimate that the Bureau spends about seven million dollars per year maintaining a network of 1,500 paid informers.

FBI Director Clarence Kelley stated in 1975 that the burglaries of the SWP offices were discontinued permanently in 1966. After a Justice Department probe began, Kelley reversed this statement and admitted that "a limited number" of burglaries had been committed in 1972 and 1973. That did not end the matter. In July 1976, Denver, Colorado police arrested Timothy Redfearn, who had just gained entry surreptitiously—in what the FBI calls a "black bag job"—to the SWP's Denver office. Documents later released show that Redfearn became an FBI informer in 1970 and broke into an apartment occupied by SWP members and into the party's bookstore. According to Bureau papers, Redfearn was dropped as an informer in 1975 because of his arrest on a burglary charge and because he was undergoing psychiatric care in hospital for depression. Nevertheless, he was reactivated as an informer later in 1975 and FBI reports consistently evaluated him as an "emotionally stable" person who provided "excellent" or "very good" information. This FBI informant's responsibilities extended beyond illegal actions against the SWP. In February 1977 Redfearn, then serving a ten-year sentence for burglary, admitted that in 1976 he broke into a house belonging to a Colorado Congresswoman on instructions from the Denver FBI office. He said he was paid $4,100 by two FBI agents to stop him from telling a grand jury details of FBI involvement in the affair. Redfearn made the charges to a high-level justice department delegation investigating illegal activities of the FBI. He said the purpose of the burglary was to obtain documents for the Bureau's file on Representative Patricia Schroeder, a Colorado Democrat.

Documents disclosing illegal FBI activities continue to be released as a result of the damage suit launched by the SWP, through other individual law suits and through the recently enacted Freedom of Information Act. It has been revealed, for example, that the New York City office of the FBI recommended commendations and cash incentives for a team of six agents who committed 15 illegal burglaries of the SWP office in that city in 1964 and 1965. The documents praised the agents for "constant alertness, swift action, sound judgement and great discretion" in obtaining the information.

The FBI has refused to admit officially its policy of rewarding agents for illegal break-ins, though in the past FBI sources have indicated to reporters that such bonuses for illegal activities were indeed given. Former senior Bureau officials have said that specially-trained squads, carrying no Bureau identification and prepared "to take a fall" if arrested, were used to enter the premises of various political groups to photograph or steal documents that could not be obtained legally without a search warrant.

These illegal FBI activities were components of spy programs with special code names, like those used by the domestic surveillance programs of the CIA, the military and the Internal Revenue Service. The FBI has used VIDEM, STUDEN, COMINFIL, and COINTELPRO to name only those about which some information has been made public. Of these, COINTELPRO, the FBI's counterintelligence program, was perhaps the most far-reaching.

Beginning in 1956, the most senior officials in the FBI authorized a coordinated program of infiltration, disruption and propaganda. COINTELPRO was launched at least partially because of the FBI's frustration with U.S. Supreme Court rulings, which throughout the middle and late 1950s had begun to limit the government's power to proceed overtly against dissident groups. For the next 15 years, until the threat of public disclosure curtailed the program in 1971, the FBI conducted, in the words of the Senate's Church committee, "a sophisticated vigilante operation aimed squarely at preventing the exercise of First Amendment rights of speech and association..." by those whom the agency perceived as "threats to the existing political and social order".

The committee also noted that more than half of the approved COINTELPRO operations were directed against the Communist Party. The Bureau interpreted "subversive" affiliation broadly, however, and COINTELPRO operations expanded to include the prevention of "communist infiltration" in mass organizations as diverse as the United Farm Workers Organizing Committee, the Students for a Democratic Society, the American Friends Service Committee, the Christian Nationalist Crusade, the National Association for the Advancement of Colored People, the women's liberation movement and the Boy Scouts.

FBI witnesses before the Church committee testified that COINTELPRO was intended to protect national security and to prevent violence. The committee's report found that the Bureau's efforts went beyond this mandate and that "the unexpressed major premise of much of COINTELPRO is that the Bureau has a role in maintaining the existing social order and...combatting those who threaten that order."

Since, as the committee noted, "many Americans and domestic groups subjected to investigation were not suspected of criminal activity," the FBI used *agents provocateurs* to create criminal activity where none had existed. One FBI operative who had directed an anti-war group's raid on a draft board office described the process:

> I taught them everything they knew...how to cut glass and open windows without making any noise...how to open file cabinets without a key...how to climb ladders easily and walk on the edge of the roof without falling....I began to feel like the Pied Piper.

In order to chill the right of free speech and to further disrupt organizations, the FBI actively fostered the suspicions of penetration by informers. A favourite COINTELPRO tactic to achieve this goal was the planting of "snitch jackets"—false information or documents indicating that a loyal member of an organization had cooperated with the police. In this way the Bureau created mistrust among members of the targeted organization and rendered loyal individuals ineffective while at the same time diverting suspicion from real FBI informers.

Addressing the Church committee, FBI agent George Moore, supervisor of the Racial Intelligence Section, described the agency's reliance on spreading paranoia:

> If you have good intelligence you know what [an organization] is going to do, you can seed distrust, sow misinformation. The same technique is used in the foreign field. The same technique...misinformation, disruption, is used in domestic groups.

These techniques were successfully employed in the FBI's attacks on minority group organizations and leaders who challenged existing American racial policies and practices. Such groups, predictably, received the harshest FBI treatment in part because J. Edgar Hoover was personally committed to preventing the success of the civil rights movement, the growth of black groups and the rise of a militant black "messiah" such as Martin Luther King, Stokely Carmichael or Malcolm X.

In November, 1968 Hoover ordered his agents to employ COINTELPRO techniques to "fully capitalize" on an atmosphere replete with "threats of murder and reprisals" that existed among black nationalist groups in California. He suggested in particular, "hard hitting" actions against the Black Panther Party in order to "exploit all avenues of creating further dissension with the ranks of the BPP". Two months later two young Black Panthers were shot and killed by members of a rival organization. A memo to Hoover from the San Diego, California office indicates that such losses to the BPP were consistent with FBI goals:

> Shootings, beatings and a high degree of unrest continues to prevail in the ghetto area of San Diego. Although no specific counterintelligence action can be credited with contributing to this over-all situation, *it is felt that a substantial amount of unrest is directly attributable to this program* [emphasis added].

During and following the COINTELPRO period, actual police attacks on California BPP members were extremely common. In sworn testimony, former Los Angeles police informer Louis Tackwood stated:

> During this period the police were shooting Panthers left and right, in cars or wherever they could catch them. They were shooting them down as fast as they could find them, and the verdict would always be "justifiable homicide".

This testimony was given at the 1976 trial of the San Quentin Six—black prisoners allegedly involved in an attempted escape from San Quentin maximum security prison. Black leader George Jackson and a prison guard were killed in the incident. Tackwood stated that he had personally participated in a conspiracy of law enforcement officials to assassinate members of the Black Panther Party.

On the Chicago front of the FBI's war against the Panthers, a letter was sent to Jeff Fort, leader of the Blackstone Rangers, a rival of the Black Panthers. The letter said a "hit" had been ordered on Fort and suggested "I know what I'd do if I was you." The forged letter aimed "to intensify the degree of animosity between the two groups... which could disrupt the BPP or lead to reprisals against its leadership" and was apparently sent as a result of instructions from FBI headquarters. The Chicago field office had been told to submit every two weeks, "imaginative proposals aimed at crippling the Black Panther Organization".

In November 1969, the FBI assisted the Chicago police in the third of a series of armed raids on Black Panther Party leaders. In the pre-dawn attack on their apartment, BPP leaders Fred Hampton and Mark Clark were shot to death. Their parents and seven survivors of the raid subsequently filed a seven million dollar damage suit against the police and the FBI, alleging that the Bureau deliberately planned and executed the raid to put an end to the BPP in Chicago. A federal grand jury which met in 1970 returned no indictments but concluded that police reports of the raid were so contradictory that it appeared the police had participated in a cover-up. Subsequent evidence revealed that Black Panther chairman Fred Hampton's bodyguard was a paid FBI informant who supplied the Bureau with a detailed floor plan of the apartment where Hampton and Clark slept, including the notation, "Hampton sleeps here".

During the 4:45 a.m. raid on December 4, 1969, teams of Chicago police armed with automatic weapons riddled the apartment with gunfire; 99 shots were fired in all, only one of which came from a Panther weapon. Within minutes, Mark Clark lay dead on the living room floor, Fred Hampton was shot to death in his sleep and several other occupants of the apartment were wounded.

Seven years later, the *Chicago Daily News* reported that a woman had been asked by the FBI to drug Hampton prior to the raid. According to the *News*, Maria Fischer said she refused to administer a drug to Hampton, but evidence exists that *someone* did: prior to Ms. Fischer's statement, an independent inquiry by former U.S. Attorney General Ramsay Clark found that Hampton had received such a large dose of drugs that he did not awaken when police began shooting into the apartment.

The Church committee's investigation of the FBI's attacks on the Black Panthers, the Socialist Workers Party and Martin Luther King, Jr., and the many other glimpses it provided into the seamy and frightening world of the secret police are by no means exhaustive. The committee did not investigate the FBI campaign against the American Indian Movement, despite strong evidence that it too was subjected to the full range of COINTELPRO techniques. The committee's plans to look into this aspect of the FBI's activities were diverted by the shooting deaths of two FBI agents on the Pine Ridge Reservation on June 26, 1975. The Bureau supporters argued, successfully, that it could not afford to have its hands tied by a congressional investigation while attempting to solve the crime.

What the Church committee thereby failed to document was a long and intensive COINTELPRO-style campaign against AIM which included FBI intervention in the trials of AIM leaders following Wounded Knee and a continuing strategy of infiltration, disruption, intimidation and provocation. The same pattern of terrorism and one-sided law enforcement which Martin Luther King exposed in the southern states and which decimated the urban-based Black Panthers also prevailed on a midwestern Indian reservation where AIM supporters were killed and the movement's effectiveness shattered.

5/From Battlefield to Courtroom

In April 1971, a few weeks after a break-in at the FBI's Media, Pennsylvania office had resulted in the public exposure of COIN-TELPRO, FBI director J. Edgar Hoover sent a carefully worded letter to his subordinates ordering an end to the program, but with this qualification:

> In exceptional instances where it is considered counterintelligence is warranted, recommendations should be submitted to the Bureau under the individual case caption to which it pertains. These recommendations will be considered on an individual basis.

What Hoover was ending was only the use of the label COINTEL-PRO and its system of reporting counterintelligence work; the tactics and the philosophy underlying the program remained unchanged. In the 1970s the FBI continued to use methods similar to those it had used against Martin Luther King in the 1960s. One of the target groups was the American Indian Movement.

Groups like the Black Panther Party and AIM "were targeted for surveillance at least in part because of their political attitudes", according to Senator Frank Church, chairman of the Senate Select Committee on Intelligence. In the case of the American Indian Movement, the political attitudes that the Bureau apparently found objectionable included its demand that Indian people be granted their civil rights under American law and its insistence that the United States honour the treaties it had made with Indian people and acknowledge the rights granted by those treaties. The first evidence of FBI surveillance of AIM surfaced during the Trail of Broken Treaties march on Washington in 1972. The FBI campaign was stepped up after the occupation of Wounded Knee; AIM then became a candidate for all manner of Bureau surveillance and counterintelligence activities, including one of the Bureau's major weapons—the selective use and misuse of the judicial system.

The occupation of Wounded Knee resulted in 562 arrests by federal authorities alone and indictments against 185 persons by federal grand juries. State and tribal charges added to these numbers. The seemingly endless charges included arson and larceny in relation to the occupation of the Wounded Knee trading post; assault and kidnapping; aiding and abetting in these crimes; and taking part in conspiracies to commit them. There were many lesser charges. Some individuals were arrested for having tried to drive to South Dakota with food and clothing destined for the occupiers and were taken into custody hundreds of miles from the occupied village.

Out of this plethora of charges and arrests, the grand jury indictment of AIM leaders Russell Means and Dennis Banks became the test case for both the government and for AIM. When the trial opened on January 8, 1974 in St. Paul, Minnesota, the two men faced grand jury indictments on ten counts for their roles in the occupation. As leaders they were held responsible for all the crimes allegedly committed during the siege, whether they personally took part in them or not. During the trial half of these charges were dismissed for lack of evidence. When the government rested its case in July, there remained charges of conspiracy in the seizure of Wounded Knee, theft from the village trading post and three counts of assaulting federal officers.

At no time did Banks or Means deny that on February 27, 1973 they and about 200 supporters had taken over the village of Wounded Knee and held it for 71 days. They defended their action on the basis of the 1868 Fort Laramie Treaty which recognizes the Sioux tribe as a sovereign jurisdiction with control over law and justice within the borders of the reservation. It was the first time that treaty law had been invoked as a defense in what the U.S. government considered a criminal trial.

The two AIM leaders laid counter-charges: they accused the Bureau of Indian Affairs of misusing funds designated for reservation residents and they charged the elected leaders of the Oglala Sioux tribe with using a "goon squad" to conduct a reign of terror on the reservation. From the beginning, the prosecution insisted that it was a straightforward criminal trial, a larceny-conspiracy-assault case, and that permitting present laws to be broken in order to rectify past wrongs would lead to anarchy. The two defendants argued that their intention had not been to break American law, but to uphold treaty law.

The 1868 Sioux Treaty remained an issue when the case finally went to the jury eight months later. Federal Court Judge Fred Nichol told the jury that the treaty was in evidence before it and that it could consider possible violations of it. He also instructed the jurors that the treaty was not a legal defence, saying: "Even if the defendants acted out of the highest moral principles, such motives do not confer immunity from criminal prosecution. Purity of motive alone will not negate criminal intent."

Throughout the trial, Banks and Means also sought acquittal on the basis of government misconduct in the case. Defence allegations of government wrongdoing resulted in six evidentiary hearings which lasted hundreds of hours. These hearings, held out of the presence of the jury to rule on the admissibility of certain evidence, turned into a trial of the FBI as numerous agents took the witness stand to explain and defend their actions.

One such hearing occurred early in the trial when Joe Pourrier, the Oglala Sioux manager of the Bison State Telephone Company, testified that he had installed an illegal wiretap at Wounded Knee on written orders from federal agents. During the five-week hearing that followed, Judge Nichol ruled that the FBI had "obliterated" a piece of evidence, prompting a precedent-setting action: Nichol ordered the FBI's entire file on Wounded Knee to be brought before the court. Only then was it learned that the FBI had *315,000 separate* file classifications on the case, with many of the individual classifications running from 600 pages to many times that size. The revelation prompted Judge Nichol to remark; "If this government falls it won't be because of subversion. It will topple under the weight of its own paperwork."

Later, when one of the FBI agents who had done some of the telephone monitoring at Wounded Knee admitted under oath that he had violated the electronic surveillance law by being party to a wiretap not authorized by the court, Banks and Means tried to place him under citizen's arrest in the presence of the judge. Judge Nichol would not allow an arrest to take place in his courtroom, however, so the defendants and their supporters chased the agent through the streets of downtown St. Paul. They didn't catch him; but the incident and others like it made it clear that the two AIM leaders were not the only accused in the St. Paul courtroom.

In a closely related portion of testimony, Joseph Trimbach, the special agent in charge of the FBI regional office in Minneapolis, told the court he knew nothing of the Wounded Knee wiretap. When the defence produced a wiretap affidavit in Trimbach's own name, Judge Nichol angrily rebuked the FBI official and indicated out of court that Trimbach had perjured himself. Defence attorney William Kunstler (who had previously defended the Chicago Seven charged in connection with the Days of Rage that accompanied the 1968 Democratic convention) charged Trimbach with perjury and demanded that he be prosecuted. No charges were laid, however. "They simply don't prosecute people in the FBI, even though scores of them have been involved in illegal activities of all sorts," Kunstler charged. The defence then asked that the charges against Means and Banks be dropped. The motion was denied.

In another incident, the entire testimony of a witness had to be erased from the record because the government violated a court order requiring it to reveal to the defence all the exculpatory evidence in its possession. Despite the court order, the prosecution withheld a written statement in which the witness completely contradicted all that he had said in court.

Yet another evidentiary hearing occurred as a result of the last minute testimony of Louis Moves Camp, a 22-year-old Oglala Sioux whom the prosecution produced as a witness after it had already rested its case in July. Moves Camp testified during the government's rebuttal in the final days of the lengthy trial. His three-day-long account of what he had seen at Wounded Knee was the only real evidence linking Banks and Means to the grand jury charges. One day's research by the defence produced witnesses whose testimony refuted everything that Moves Camp had said. Evidence showed he had been in California at the time he was supposed to have witnessed the alleged crimes. The government could have found these witnesses as easily as the defence did, attorney William Kunstler charged. It did not; instead it allowed Moves Camp to perjure himself for three days.

The evidentiary hearing resulted from defence allegations that the FBI had unduly influenced the dropping of rape charges against the witness. While awaiting his turn on the witness stand, Moves Camp had been kept by FBI agents David Price and Ray Williams in a Wisconsin border town. During this time Moves Camp allegedly raped a young girl, who pressed charges against him. After the alleged crime occurred, Moves Camp was taken out of the jurisdiction by the agents and ensconced in their hotel suite. The agents let it be known that they did not want charges pressed against the young man, defence attorney Kenneth Tilsen charged. The very fact that Moves Camp had obvious ties with the agents would have deterred local authorities from laying charges even if the agents had said nothing, Tilsen claimed. During a hearing into the affair, an incident occurred which Judge Nichol later called "bizarre": two armed FBI agents were discovered eavesdropping on the testimony of a witness testifying in camera. Judge Nichol immediately adjourned the proceedings and called the agents into his chambers for a tongue-lashing.

There were frequent dramatic outbursts during the trial. Defence attorneys William Kunstler, Mark Lane (author of the John F. Kennedy assassination book, *Rush to Judgment*) and Kenneth Tilsen were ejected from the courtroom on the opening day of arguments. In June, Lane was jailed briefly for contempt of court after heated questioning of an FBI informer. During the questioning of yet another FBI informer in late August, a fist-fighting, mace-spraying brawl broke out between marshals and the defen-

Mary Ellen Pictou and her daughter Anna Mae   *Photo: courtesy Rebecca Julian*

A school picture, 1956   *Photo: courtesy R. Julian*

The house at Shubenacadie   *Photo: courtesy R. Julian*

Rebecca, Francis, Anna Mae and their mother with the family's first
Christmas tree   *Photo: courtesy R. Julian*

Anna Mae in Boston   *Photo: courtesy R. Julian*

Anna Mae Aquash and Mark Silver
modelling Nishnawba fashions and jewellery at the National Arts Centre, Ottawa,
May 1974   *CP Photo*

Nogeeshik and Anna Mae Aquash, during the 1973 Wounded Knee occupation, talking with medicine man Wallace Black Elk at the site of the 1890
Wounded Knee massacre   *Kevin Barry McKiernan*

Anna Mae using a golf club to dig a bunker inside Wounded Knee, April 1973
K.B. McKiernan

Members of the reservation goon squad manning an illegal roadblock used to prevent court-ordered food and medical supplies from reaching Wounded Knee *K.B. McKiernan*

Anna Mae and Nogeeshik Aquash after their traditional Sioux wedding ceremony at Wounded Knee, April 12, 1973   *K.B. McKiernan*

U.S. National Guard soldiers at a roadblock outside the occupied Alexian Brothers Novitiate near Gresham, Wisconsin, January 1975. Anna Mae Aquash operated a radio communications unit on the Menominee Reservation near this roadblock.   *K.B. McKiernan*

The body of Joe Stuntz, the 18-year-old Indian killed in the June 26, 1975 shoot-out on the Pine Ridge Reservation   *K.B. McKiernan*

Celia Jumping Bull, whose home was damaged by FBI gunfire on June 26, 1975. She holds portraits of her son and two nephews, all killed while serving with the U.S. military overseas. *K.B. McKiernan*

A federal agent standing over the body of Joe Stuntz
K.B. McKiernan

The Jumping Bull property right after the June 26 shoot-out   *K.B. McKiernan*

An FBI agent involved in the Pine Ridge manhunt after the June 26
shoot-out   *K.B. McKiernan*

Helicopter used by FBI agents during the Pine Ridge manhunt   *K.B.*
McKiernan

An FBI agent involved in the Pine Ridge manhunt
K.B. McKiernan

The bluff over which Anna Mae's body was pushed. The body was found at the foot of the bluff between the two darkened patches of earth. *K.B. McKiernan*

Roger Amiotte at the site where he discovered the body of Anna Mae Aquash
on February 24, 1976   *K.B. McKiernan*

The body of Anna Mae Aquash wrapped in an American Indian Movement
flag   *K.B. McKiernan*

Anna Mae's body being carried to the grave   *K.B. McKiernan*

Mourners at Anna Mae's funeral   *K.B. McKiernan*

The funeral of Anna Mae Aquash, March 1976   *K.B. McKiernan*

dants' supporters in the spectators' gallery. Both Lane and Kunstler were jailed overnight as a result. At one point Lane said he was assaulted by a United States marshal who punched him in the face, causing his glasses to fly 20 feet across the room. "I'm going to work you over, you son of a bitch," the marshal told his victim. "I'm going to work you over so that no one will recognize you." A group of marshals standing nearby later claimed they had witnessed no such incident.

On September 12, the jury left the St. Paul courtroom to begin its deliberations. The alternate jurors were then released from their oaths, and they let it be known that the regular jurors might well acquit the AIM leaders. After just eight hours of deliberations, however, a 55-year-old female juror was incapacitated by a heart attack. U.S. law provides for an automatic mistrial in such cases, unless both the prosecution and the defence agree to go ahead with an abbreviated jury. The defence was willing; the prosecution was not.

Throughout the trial the defence had maintained that the two AIM leaders were on trial for their political beliefs. Statements made by chief prosecutor R.D. Hurd near the end of the trial seemed to confirm that view. Before the jury began its deliberations, and before the alternate jurors had made known that the predominant inclination was for acquittal, prosecutor Hurd said his job was "not to get a conviction" but "to prosecute the case...to represent society and get all the evidence that is fair and just before the jury". Hurd said his job was essentially over once the jury began its deliberations. When the juror fell ill, however, Hurd became unwilling to go ahead with an 11-person jury because the alternate jurors' statements indicated that "our chances of getting a conviction are not very good". He avoided a final decision on the matter, however, apparently because he was awaiting orders from highly-placed Washington Justice Department officials—indicating that the Nixon-Ford administration attached considerable political importance to the outcome of the trial.

Prosecutor Hurd said, "It's important to obtain a conviction in this case because of the effect it's going to have on the other

Wounded Knee trials, other defendants and perhaps on the basic question of what methods and means are available to people seeking redress." There were some 100 Wounded Knee cases still pending. The final decision about continuing with the abbreviated jury could come from the Attorney General himself, Hurd stated, though he thought it more likely that lower-ranking Justice Department officials would be involved in the decision. "The Attorney General is not in a position to determine what the chances of getting a conviction would be."

Before the Washington officials reached their decision, the issue became irrelevant. The defence presented Judge Nichol with a last-minute motion for acquittal based on repeated government misconduct during the long and costly trial. More than eight months had elapsed, hundreds of exhibits had been filed and testimony from witnesses had filled thousands of pages of transcript. The trial had cost an estimated $750,000. Judge Nichol, angered by the prosecution's reluctance to continue with an abbreviated jury, accepted the defence motion.

In dismissing the charges, Judge Nichol delivered a blistering 75-minute attack on assistant U.S. attorney R.D. Hurd. The chief prosecutor, he said, was more interested in obtaining a conviction than in seeing justice done. He had not been a servant of the law. Judge Nichol accused him of collaborating with the FBI to quash the Louis Moves Camp rape investigation in August. He said Hurd had lied to the court and added: "The U.S. attorney may strike hard blows, but he is not at liberty to strike foul ones."

Judge Nichol also cited the illegal intervention of the armed forces during the Wounded Knee occupation as a contributing factor in his decision to dismiss the charges. The Pentagon had covertly supplied more than $300,000 in arms, personnel and assistance to civilian police agencies during the siege, contravening U.S. federal law, which states that such intervention can occur only by presidential proclamation. "We don't want the military running the civil affairs in this country, or having anything to do with the execution of laws," he said.

The judge reserved his harshest criticism for the FBI, which, in committing numerous illegal acts had "stooped to a low state".

FBI misconduct, he noted, had also resulted in the dismissal of charges in another AIM trial at which he presided—the trial of those involved in the Twin Cities Naval Air Station takeover in 1971. Said Nichol, "I used to think the FBI was one of the best organizations ever to come down the pike, but now I think it's deteriorated, deteriorated badly." Nichol was referring not only to the St. Paul trial, but also to the Watergate scandals and the lawlessness that had recently forced the resignation of President Richard Nixon, when he concluded: "It's been a bad year for justice, in this country, a bad year for justice."

Dennis Banks and Russell Means viewed their acquittal—later upheld in appellate court—as a vindication of their treaty rights. "This shows that people can stand up," Russell Means said after the trial. "It shows Indian people all over the country that we can stand up for our rights and people will recognize it." Judge Nichol's ruling upheld not Banks' and Means' treaty rights, but their constitutional rights to a fair trial under United States law. It affirmed their freedom to speak and organize on behalf of their chosen cause; but it did not guarantee them freedom from police harassment in their work.

The FBI, shamed in court and faced with the acquittals of the two men because of its own misconduct, did not abandon its COINTELPRO-style campaign against AIM, but intensified it. From the Bureau's perspective the eight months in court had not been wasted, despite the judicial rebuke. Throughout 1974, the energies of AIM leaders and supporters were devoted to supporting the trial effort and raising funds for the defence. The defence was the collective effort of AIM members, WKLDOC legal workers and attorneys, and thousands of Indian people and other sympathizers, who showed their support either by observing the courtroom proceedings or by sending what money they could afford. As long as they were in court, the AIM leaders could do little other work. As one AIM supporter noted, "Being a movement leader is in itself a 120-hour-a-week job. You can't do it while you're in court and you can't do it between speaking engagements and lecture tours." Yet the former often necessitated the latter.

Tying up the AIM leaders in costly and time-consuming court battles was a strategy that the FBI continued to use successfully. The outcome of the 562 Wounded Knee arrests and 185 indictments made it clear that charges against and arrests of AIM members often had little to do with the likelihood of obtaining convictions. In 1974, 78 per cent of indictments that resulted in trials in the U.S. district court's eighth circuit resulted in convictions. The 185 Wounded Knee indictments resulted in only 15 convictions, 11 for felonies—a conviction rate of 7.7 per cent.

These harassing prosecutions based on insubstantial evidence continued in use against AIM members after the St. Paul trial of Dennis Banks and Russell Means. In March 1975 for example, Means was charged in the March 2, 1975 shooting death of Martin Montileux in a Scenic, South Dakota bar, although with his dying breath Montileux had told police officers, "It was not Russell Means who shot me." Means was acquitted after a short trial, making it the seventh occasion on which he had been charged with a violent crime without evidence sufficient for a conviction.

Another of the legal weapons frequently used by the FBI to serve its counterintelligence program is the grand jury, with its power of subpoena. The subpoena, which usually arrives by the hand of an FBI agent, compels the party named to submit to questioning behind closed doors, without benefit of legal counsel. The grand jury is a panel of citizens designated to investigate alleged violations of the law and to determine whether the evidence is sufficient to warrant a trial. It was originally conceived as a protection against politically-motivated prosecutions, with the citizens' panel serving as a check on the powers of the appointed district attorneys and judges. The grand jury subpoena can become, however, a licence for the FBI to go fishing in otherwise protected areas of free speech and association. The secrecy of grand jury questioning, originally intended to protect witnesses, can become an instrument to harass them.

The interrogation is usually based on investigations made by the FBI, and the supposedly independent grand jury is often "guided" by agents or district attorneys. The witness caught in a politically-inspired grand jury investigation faces a cruel dilemma.

Those who invoke the Fifth Amendment as a constitutional protection against self-incrimination are often "given" immunity from prosecution and forced to testify. Non-cooperation leads to contempt citations and a jail term for the life of the grand jury—usually 18 months. Even pro forma compliance in the secret interrogations brands the witness, in the eyes of associates, as a possible police informer. This is particularly true among those American Indians who believe that treaty sovereignty supercedes the powers of the grand jury; many native Americans have been caught in this double bind.

In one such case, Joanna LeDeaux invoked Oglala Sioux treaty rights in refusing to answer grand jury questions following the June 26, 1975 shoot-out on Pine Ridge Reservation described later in this book. She complained of severe FBI harassment of herself, her son and her ex-husband. Refusing to testify, she was jailed for contempt. In sentencing her, South Dakota Judge Andrew Bogue stated, "The keys to the cell are in your mouth." LeDeaux gave birth to her second son while in prison.

Angie and Ivis Long Visitor were also jailed for contempt at about the same time. They were refused bail pending an appeal. When the Supreme Court also refused them bail, the couple relented and testified before the grand jury: they had three children under four years of age and the threatened term in a Rapid City, South Dakota jail was too high a price to pay. Their testimony contained no information relevant to the government. However, even their reluctant cooperation with the FBI and federal prosecutors produced rumours which caused them heartache upon their return to the reservation. Eleven-year-old Jimmy Zimmerman was more fortunate. Picked up by the FBI and taken to the grand jury, he pleaded his treaty rights and stubbornly refused to testify without a lawyer. The federal prosecutor judiciously released him without pressing a contempt charge.

Such incidents were the subject of a Lakota Treaty Council's meeting with President Gerald Ford in November 1975. The old chiefs and tribal headsmen, who represent the traditional Sioux followers of the 1868 Fort Laramie Treaty, protested not only the abuses of the South Dakota grand jury system, but the continued harassment activities of the FBI on their reservation. They drew to the President's attention the 54 violent deaths which had occurred on the reservation in two and a half years following the Wounded Knee occupation and noted that most of the victims were American Indian Movement supporters. Louis Bad Wound told Mr. Ford that the FBI agents were "playing out their childhood fantasies about cowboys and Indians—only those are real bullets and we're real Indians". The meeting was brief and the President told the delegation he was "greatly encouraged by the kind of responsibility that all of you have shown as leaders of the Sioux tribe".

Senator James Abourezk, a South Dakota Democrat, made numerous criticisms of FBI conduct on Pine Ridge to representatives of the President, but was unable to obtain any action to remedy the lawlessness on the reservation. Abourezk believes his criticisms made his family the object of FBI retaliation. In May 1976, Abourezk's son Charles, a 22-year-old college student living on the reservation, was identified in an FBI teletype designed to create a hostile attitude among lawmen in their dealings with Indian people. The teletype, sent to thousands of law enforcement agencies across the United States, alleged that Charlie Abourezk was storing guns in his home for use in violent attacks by Indians during the July 4, 1976 bicentennial celebration. It indicated that he was holding the weapons for use by AIM "dog soldiers" who were planning to assassinate the South Dakota governor, burn farm land, snipe at motorists travelling on the interstate freeway, raid the state prison, bomb the state capitol and ransack the BIA building. The "dog soldiers", the FBI message asserted, would shoot at police officers who stopped them on the highway and lay ambushes for lawmen. FBI director Clarence Kelley later admitted that the dog soldier alert had no basis in fact and could not explain why it had been issued. In a Washington, D.C. press conference, Senator Abourezk called the FBI tactics "damned outrageous practices". Demanding a congressional investigation, the South Dakota Democrat charged, "It smacks of a total set-up that these unfounded, unverified reports are given such widespread distribution."

The incident occurred in 1976, when the extent of the FBI's

COINTELPRO-style campaign against AIM had become more clearly delineated. In September 1974, when Dennis Banks and Russell Means were released following the Wounded Knee trial, the dimensions of the attack on AIM could only be estimated. It was not until six months later that AIM discovered that its chief of security during the trial was a well-paid FBI operative. Only then did it become obvious that chief prosecutor R.D. Hurd and the FBI's senior regional official, Joseph Trimbach, had perjured themselves in court to keep that identity secret; and that the spy they sought to protect was no ordinary informer but an experienced and dangerous *agent provocateur.*

6/Douglass Durham, Agent Provocateur

On July 7, 1976 FBI Director Clarence Kelley asserted under oath that "The American Indian Movement is a movement which has fine goals, and has as its general consideration of what needs to be done, something that is worthwhile; and it is not tabbed by us as an un-American, subversive or otherwise objectionable organization."

The FBI chief's sworn statement was greeted with amazement by members and supporters of the American Indian Movement: it seemed that either Kelley was not telling the truth, or he did not know what the agency he led was doing.

A more plausible indication of how government officials, particularly the FBI, viewed the organization, came from Senator James Eastland, head of the Senate Subcommittee on Internal Security. Two months after Kelley's statement, the Eastland committee issued a report declaring that AIM was a "frankly revolutionary operation which is committed to violence, calls for the arming of American Indians, has cached explosives and illegally purchased arms, plans kidnappings and whose opponents have been eliminated in the manner of the Mafia...."

AIM's main activities, according to Senator Eastland, consisted of running an "underground railroad" to smuggle weapons and warriors between the United States and Canada. Eastland attempted to show links between AIM and international terrorist organizations, as well as links with communist groups. An ardent supporter of the methods used by U.S. intelligence agencies, Eastland based his entire report and its apocalyptic warnings on the testimony of a single FBI witness—Douglass Durham.

The American Indian Movement had long been aware that it was under FBI surveillance. Paid informers testified at the trial of Dennis Banks and Russell Means and there were many others: John Arellano had pretended to be a "right-on" Indian and ardent AIM supporter during the Trail of Broken Treaties occupation of BIA headquarters in Washington; a white couple with a long history of spying on political groups, Jill and Fred "Gi" Schaeffer infiltrated the Wounded Knee Legal Defence/Offense Committee and made a systematic effort to disrupt it and to entrap AIM members and supporters until they were finally expelled; erstwhile AIM member Bernie Morning Gun admitted to receiving $1,500 from the FBI for providing information about Minneapolis-St. Paul AIM. Morning Gun was asked to write personality profiles of various AIM members and provide information on the defence strategy in trials related to the Wounded Knee occupation. The FBI wanted to know such details as whether actor Marlon Brando was providing bail money for the defendants. Agents told Morning Gun that AIM "was getting guns from Canada" and offered him an additional $5,000 if he could obtain information on weapons. The FBI promised Morning Gun a change of identity and a new life in a distant location; but he eventually went underground on his own after confessing his spying activities and travelling with AIM members speaking on FBI activities before college audiences.

As various individuals proved, it was not difficult to infiltrate AIM. The organization was proud of its non-bureaucratic style and openness. There were no formal membership procedures and anyone could call himself or herself a member. The loosely structured organization had no effective method of keeping out informers. When such persons were identified, a circular was sent around stating that the individual had been expelled from AIM for conduct "unbecoming to a member" or similarly vague wording. One reason why security remained ineffective was that the person whose job it was to weed out government informers and who authorized the incriminating circulars, was himself an operative for the FBI. AIM's security director was Douglass Durham, an experienced informer and provocateur.

During the two years in which he operated undetected in AIM, Durham rapidly gained access to the top leaders by performing a variety of useful services with skill and imagination. In doing so, he won the friendship and confidence of Dennis Banks, a relationship which protected him from all but the most indisputable charges of deception and treachery.

A white man with a smattering of Indian blood, Durham contrived his Indian appearance by dying his hair black, wearing contact lenses and adopting the AIM-style dress—ribbon shirts, turquoise and silver jewellery and beadwork. He brought valuable skills to the organization: he was a photographer and pilot and had abilities as an administrator and organizer. He proved to be persuasive, even eloquent, in pleading AIM's cause with the church groups that provided essential funds. Durham was what one WKLDOC attorney called "an attractive package".

Durham's association with AIM began when he went into Wounded Knee as a photographer for an obscure paper, *Pax Today*, now believed to have been a government front for intelligence gathering. He took photos of the Wounded Knee occupiers and their defences during a five-hour stint inside the village and then, according to his story, offered the material to the FBI. He told AIM investigators he accepted the FBI assignment only after an agent challenged him, saying, "You could go right to the top of that organization if you wanted to."

It is possible however, that Durham was much more than a freelance information peddler subsequently hired by the FBI. His undercover work for the Bureau is suspected by some to have been a cover for his real role—that of a domestic CIA operative. The CIA's domestic program—operation CHAOS—was an illegal spying and disruption campaign against AIM and 13 other American groups and was revealed by the report of the Rockefeller Commission inquiry into that organization in 1975.

Durham has a history of involvement in known CIA operations, according to Paula Giese, who researched his past after his identity as an FBI spy became known. Following a four-year stint in the Marines in the late 1950s, Durham underwent a CIA training course and later provided logistical support to ex-patriate Cubans taking part in the 1961 Bay of Pigs invasion. Giese's research also revealed that Durham was fired from his job as a Des Moines, Iowa patrolman in 1964, after a fight with his pregnant wife over his alleged activities as a pimp and burglar. His wife died on July 5, 1964, shortly after the fight.

From then until he surfaced as an FBI informer during the occupation of Wounded Knee, Durham allegedly developed close connections with organized crime, continuing his pimping activities and acting at times as a police informer. Durham also helped train police in various urban centres in undercover and intelligence work.

In 1972, a number of Des Moines police, including chief Wendell Nicholls, were reprimanded for their relationship with Durham, "a known or suspected receiver of stolen goods". Police rules forbade association with such persons. It was Chief Nicholls who later said, "I can't believe that with all the publicity, AIM didn't know who he was." Durham later boasted that Iowa police considered him head of the largest criminal organization in the state. Giese found that he was a man feared by politicians, police and ordinary citizens alike; they considered him "untouchable" and believe that he maintained his organized crime links when he offered his services to the FBI in 1973.

Durham's first act as an FBI informer and provocateur was to infiltrate Iowa AIM while the occupation of Wounded Knee was still underway. He destroyed the chapter and undermined the credibility of the local leader, Harvey Major, an Ojibway from Kenora, Ontario. Durham then encouraged the remaining Iowa activists to undertake a series of actions which earned them a reputation as "crazies". In one such incident, they staged an armed takeover of the Iowa office of education building, an action Durham orchestrated in secret collusion with the police. Local police cooperated with federal agents by arresting Durham along with those he had recruited for the takeover. The FBI paid his $100 fine, and Durham was free again. In a subsequent press conference Iowa AIM members prominently displayed their weapons for the media to photograph. Iowa AIM soon lost all but a handful of its supporters and was thoroughly discredited in the eyes of the public and of other AIM chapters. Durham, however, manipulated events so that he gained credibility in the eyes of the national AIM leadership.

In the fall of 1973, Dennis Banks went underground to avoid arrest and incarceration on charges stemming from the Custer incident earlier that year. He eventually turned up in the Northwest Territories, hiding out with several companions in the tiny community of Rae Lakes, 150 miles from Yellowknife. Durham was asked to fly north and meet him to provide money and set up communications between the northern village and AIM attorneys and supporters in the United States. The FBI was informed of Banks' plans, and apparently sought and obtained the cooperation of the RCMP in the North West Territories in a plan which preserved Durham's cover. Fugitive Banks was not arrested; instead police officials cut off all supplies of food and mail to the remote village, resulting in community pressure that forced the AIM contingent to leave. In the meantime, sufficient cash had been raised for Banks' bail and Durham salvaged a difficult situation by flying north to Edmonton, renting a plane and spiriting Banks illegally across the border in time to avoid forfeiting the bail already posted on related charges.

Banks was impressed by Durham's skillful manoeuvres, which seemed to have helped keep him out of the FBI's clutches. His admiration for Durham and the general climate of pursuit meant that the mechanics of Durham's achievements were not closely scrutinized. The money for the airplane rentals, for example, had been supplied in part by Los Angeles businessman George Roberts, the owner of an import-export business called Inca. Roberts, a white man, became influential in the Los Angeles chapter of AIM after the occupation of Wounded Knee and turned it into AIM's national press secretariat, which issued sometimes inflammatory press releases; but AIM knew little of his past or his motives.

When Banks and Means came to trial on the Wounded Knee charges on January 8, 1974, Durham had become AIM security director and coordinator of the WKLDOC support group. He became AIM's chief bureaucrat, taking charge of trial records and setting up the AIM national office in St. Paul. He had access to both AIM and WKLDOC bank accounts; and when the letters of support poured in from across the country, Durham had first access to the donations they contained. AIM estimates that he may have stolen as much as $100,000.

Durham's job during the eight-month trial was to ensure that no government informers were among the attorneys and legal workers who worked on the defence team. He was the only person other than the AIM attorneys, legal workers and the defendants with access to the defence strategy room, and he controlled security clearance for both the attorneys and the defence volunteers. As he later described this role, "I exercised so much control you couldn't see Dennis or Russell without going through me, you couldn't contact any other chapter without going through me and if you wanted money, you had to see me."

Early in the Banks-Means trial, in response to a defence motion, Judge Fred Nichol ordered the FBI files searched for evidence that the defence team—including the WKLDOC group—had been infiltrated. On April 3, 1974, chief prosecutor R.D. Hurd swore in an affidavit that the FBI's confidential source files had been searched and that they "contained no material which could arguably be considered as evidence of the invasion of the defense legal camp". After Durham was publicly exposed as an FBI informer, Hurd admitted that he had been told by the FBI that an informant "very close to one of the defendants" had been sitting in on the lawyer-client meetings but that the informant had been instructed to report only about planned violence. In other words, Durham sat in on defence preparations for the trial but never reported to his employer! According to Hurd, the informant's name had been deleted from the file.

During the Banks-Means trial, Joseph Trimbach, head of the Minneapolis area office of the FBI, testified that there were no government informers in the defence camp. Trimbach said in a 1975 pre-trial hearing that he had not known that Durham was an informer. One of his agents however, admitted having nearly 50 contacts with Durham during the trial.

Durham himself told the Eastland committee that he couldn't help overhearing defence strategy. "If Dennis and I were sitting in the room and an attorney would walk in and start talking, I couldn't jump up and say, 'I can't be here. The FBI won't allow it!'" Since Durham controlled trial security, he often found himself in what he modestly termed a "ticklish" situation.

In August of 1974, during a special trial recess, Durham piloted Banks to Kenora, Ontario, where he was to mediate between local authorities and the Indian occupiers of Anicinabe Park. The protest had begun in early August, following an Ojibway Nation Conference at which Banks was a speaker. The Ojibway Warrior Society claimed the 14-acre park as ancestral treaty land and hoped by its action to draw attention to the plight of area Indians: almost total unemployment on the two dozen reserves in the area; a high rate of alcoholism, suicide and violent death; poor health care; and the destruction of the traditional Indian lifestyle in one generation by welfare and mercury pollution of the English-Wabigoon river system. On August 14, the occupation and the tensions it produced reached a crisis: Kenora crown attorney Ted Burton ordered those remaining in the park to leave within 24 hours while Ontario Provincial Police set up barricades and began arresting those who attempted to leave.

When Ted Burton arrived home that night he found a message asking him to call Dennis Banks. He spoke to Douglass Durham and arranged for Banks to come to Kenora to mediate the dispute. Burton later observed that Durham was a "highly intelligent" individual and an able executive officer who "gave AIM good advice". Burton reports that during the two days Banks and Durham were in Kenora, "they were like two brothers—each knew every move the other was going to make." He also recalls that Durham was obsessed with communists, an attitude with which he was partially sympathetic, but which he did not understand fully until later when Durham's cover was blown. The crown attorney denied Durham's statement to the Eastland committee in 1976 concerning a cache of weapons buried in Anicinabe Park: "All I ever saw were a couple of rusty old fowling pieces."

Burton was so impressed by Durham that he helped arrange his involvement in another Canadian Indian protest action in 1974. The Native People's Caravan had marched on Ottawa, only to become what one participant called "a peanut butter sandwich"—caught in an ugly squeeze between riot police and militant white supporters on the steps of Parliament on September 30. The leaders of the caravan subsequently occupied an old mill, which they dubbed the Native People's Embassy and called for assistance from AIM. Douglass Durham was dispatched to the scene to establish, as he put it, "better communications" between the Indians and the police, and came to be highly regarded by authorities working on the case.

In September 1974, Durham attempted to involve AIM in relief operations in Honduras (Belize) following a severe hurricane in that country. Durham wanted Dennis Banks to use his interest in reservation lands to fund a team of medics to be parachuted into the country by the Foundation for Airborne Relief of California. AIM learned the organization was a CIA front and the idea was abandoned. Next Durham wanted AIM to put up $30,000 to fund a plane chartered from Flying Tiger Airlines. When a worker in the AIM office pointed out that the airline had close ties to the CIA, this plan too was dropped. Durham finally succeeded in getting the defence department to provide a plane and a special crew.

Exactly what Durham's intentions were in these manoeuvres remains unclear. AIM had just begun to make contact with native people in South America. In many of these countries, the CIA had been active in propping up dictatorial regimes. Had Durham been successful, AIM funds would have been spent in a mission that would have linked AIM with the CIA and discredited it in the eyes of South American Indians, as well as native people in Canada and the United States.

Durham had other disruptive plans for AIM. In the fall of 1974, residents of the Rosebud Reservation, which borders Pine Ridge on the east, met to air grievances and civil rights complaints on which they hoped AIM might act. Included in their complaints were a number of charges against William Janklow, a lawyer then running as Republican candidate for the office of state attorney general. In the mid 1960s Janklow was working with the Office of Economic Opportunity (OEO) legal aid program on the Rosebud Reservation. In 1966, an accusation of rape was made against him by a young Sioux girl, Jancita Eagle Deer, who had been his family's babysitter. The complaint was investigated by both the BIA and the FBI, but no criminal charges were laid against the 27-year-old poverty lawyer.

When the complaint was revived in 1974, AIM did not intend to act on it, according to defence worker Paula Giese. The story was hard to substantiate and depended, in large part, on the testimony of Jancita Eagle Deer herself. Furthermore, both she and former BIA officers on the reservation would be difficult to locate. AIM was persuaded to involve itself in the unlikely case, however, by Douglass Durham.

Jancita Eagle Deer, once a bright, ambitious student, had dropped out of school after the alleged rape. She moved to Des Moines, Iowa, where she became a somewhat promiscuous alcoholic. She became pregnant, married and was separated, unable to control her drinking. When Durham found her, she was attempting to work out her problems but was easily intimidated and manipulated. Durham aroused AIM's interest in the case when he said, "I know where to find that girl." He then brought 22-year-old Jancita Eagle Deer to the St. Paul AIM office. He also located Peter Pitchlynn, the retired BIA officer who had originally investigated the case, and was able to acquire FBI reports which showed that the Bureau had helped quash potential charges against William Janklow. AIM then filed a successful petition to have Janklow barred from the Rosebud tribal court, to which he had been appointed as attorney by the tribal council and from which he had not resigned. The presiding judge indicated there was enough evidence to warrant a criminal prosecution of Janklow and rebuked the BIA for its failure to provide its files to the court.

Durham then arranged to have Jancita Eagle Deer make her charges on a Sioux Falls, South Dakota television program on October 31, a few days prior to the election in which Janklow was running. Janklow had campaigned on a platform of fighting AIM lawlessness and made headlines with his statement that the only effective way to deal with AIM leaders was "to put a bullet through their heads". Because the old rape charges were raised again so close to the November 2 election, Janklow was able to claim successfully that the allegations were nothing more than a crude AIM smear attempt. He was elected by a two-to-one margin.

AIM leaders now suspect that the incident was created as part of an elaborate set of plans to disrupt the organization. At about the same time, AIM was planning a demonstration to demand bail for 60-year-old Sarah Bad Heart Bull who was then appealing a one-to-five-year sentence for her part in the Custer demonstration sparked by the murder of her son. Durham tried to advance the date of the demonstration to precede the election. In California he apparently made unsuccessful attempts to persuade AIM members to kidnap Janklow.

Following her appearance on Sioux Falls television, Durham installed Jancita Eagle Deer in his St. Paul apartment. She astounded workers in the AIM office by announcing that she and Durham would marry following his recovery from a deadly illness, and she spoke of Durham's large salary as an AIM director. The women in the St. Paul office—among them Anna Mae Aquash—had for nearly a year observed Durham's exploitation and abuse of various women. By late fall his questionable activities had aroused a great deal of suspicion towards Durham. The AIM women decided to refuse him access to the national office and soon made it impossible for him to work there. "We couldn't mount an overt challenge to him," said Paula Giese, "because no one would listen to us. What we were able to do was just be intransigent." Durham left St. Paul, pilfering the AIM files before he went, and took Jancita Eagle Deer with him to Phoenix. When she tried to call her mother en route, he dragged her from a telephone booth and beat her severely. When she appeared at an AIM house in Phoenix, announcing that Durham was an informer, he beat her again. Two young AIM supporters who witnessed the incident were also beaten by Durham.

In many ways the entire Eagle Deer incident typified the way Durham worked and showed how he was able to operate for so long within an organization without being suspected. On the surface, his intervention in the Eagle Deer case would seem to have been beneficial to AIM. The incident, however, must be placed in the context of South Dakota politics, the widespread hatred and fear of AIM and the general attitudes of the white population toward Indians. Anyone who took the time to assess the situation would see clearly that a seven-year-old rape charge made by an Indian woman whose credibility could easily be challenged would not be believed by South Dakotans. Thus, while it might appear that Durham was helping AIM and taking a chance with Janklow's political career, his actions were also able to disrupt AIM.

Indian people refuse to elaborate on some of Durham's disruptive tactics as an *agent provocateur*, because this would implicate other Indians. Thus, when Durham's identity as a spy was finally revealed, AIM found it difficult to sort out what he had done to help the organization and what had been disruptive. Durham's detractors and admirers alike have noted that he sometimes seemed convincingly dedicated to AIM's goals. More than one AIM supporter has claimed that Durham's ability to pretend a friendship with AIM leaders and deep sympathy for their goals while simultaneously working toward the organization's destruction indicates a highly abnormal mental and emotional state.

In January 1975, Durham appeared at the Menominee Warrior Society occupation of the Alexian Brothers Novitiate near Gresham, Wisconsin, accompanied by the reluctant Jancita Eagle Deer. The occupation had begun on New Year's night and within hours the occupiers were exchanging gunfire with 300 local sheriffs. Anger mounted in the nearby white communities, and when the National Guard was called in, it became a buffer between the Indians and the armed and hostile Concerned Citizens Committee, later renamed the White America Movement. Upon his arrival, Durham immediately took charge of media relations and announced on national television that his room was the AIM communications centre. When telephone lines to the abbey were cut, the radio set in his room became the communications link between the abbey and the world outside. Durham handled the press and the Concerned Citizens Committee. When police members of that group learned of his background they pinpointed him as AIM's "hit-man" and assumed an AIM-Mafia connection.

The Menominee Warrior Society was badly divided over the question of AIM support. There was also considerable mistrust within the group itself. Durham was not trusted and was refused access to the abbey, but he sent in his companion, Jancita Eagle Deer, to report to him. Durham managed to establish communications with the office of Wisconsin Governor Patrick Lucy and in this venture solicited the aid of Kenora crown attorney Ted Burton, who telephoned Lucy on Durham's behalf. Burton claims that as a result the National Guard adopted a lenient policy of supplying ample food, newspapers and a television set to the occupiers—a policy which contrasted sharply with official strategy at Wounded Knee.

This strategy may well have undermined the occupation by allowing the protesters to think they were winning important concessions. Whatever its effect on the occupiers, the effect of the strategy on their opponents was quite clear. "How can they call themselves warriors when they're in there watching colour television and eating great meals?" was one common reaction. Members of the Concerned Citizens Committee, angered by what they perceived as lenient treatment by the authorities, inflamed the situation by using armed snowmobiles to stage midnight raids on the occupied abbey.

It has since been suggested that the occupation came close to being an entrapment situation for the participants. Plans for the event were apparently discussed with Durham in his St. Paul office sometime in late fall 1974. No date was set for the occupation, and some maintain that other AIM leaders attempted to dissuade the Warrior Society from the action. Testimony at the trial of Michael Sturdevant, a leader sentenced to eight years in prison for his role in the occupation, indicated that the FBI had been informed of the plans and had, prior to the event, taken complete photographs of the abbey.

Those AIM members who already mistrusted Durham grew even more suspicious of the way he ran the communications centre. Midway through the occupation, he abruptly left his motel

room and fled the Gresham area. The following day a group of
AIM members, including Anna Mae Aquash, met to discuss Durham's activities and concluded that he was a spy for the FBI. They
had no conclusive proof, nor was their opinion shared by all of the
AIM leaders. They were not surprised, however, when they observed men with headsets in the room next to Durham's, which
was still the AIM communications centre following his departure.

Their assessment of Durham was confirmed two months later
when copies of Durham's reports to the FBI were released to AIM
during pre-trial hearings related to further charges arising from
the Wounded Knee occupation. Durham was cornered by the
AIM leadership and subjected to a lengthy interrogation during
which he confessed the FBI connection and revealed details about
his background. On March 12, 1975, Durham told the story of his
spying role to a national press conference in Chicago, saying he
had come to believe that "AIM was a viable legal organization
that wasn't doing anything wrong." He said he respected Dennis
Banks as well as the organization he led and stated that he had
been paid between $800 and $1,000 per month by the FBI.

The revelation of Durham's role as an FBI operative shook
AIM to its foundations. Some of its members charged that the
leadership had been too slow in dealing with the matter, even after
documentary proof had been obtained. Dennis Banks was criticized by some for being too trusting. Because of his strategic position within the AIM defence camp, Durham's revelations
damaged the FBI's plans and its reputation, but it also served the
Bureau's larger purposes of creating still more dissension and mistrust within AIM. If a government operative could become AIM's
security director then nobody in the organization was above suspicion or beyond reproach. Were there more spies among the top
leadership? Could the judgement and decisions of the leadership
be trusted?

AIM was not rid of Douglass Durham after his role as an FBI
operative was made public. AIM investigations of his activities
revealed that he had done considerable damage to the organization, although it was impossible to follow up all the obvious leads.
The extent to which he had manipulated Jancita Eagle Deer came

fully to light only after his public confession. Three weeks later, on April 4, 1975, she was struck and killed while wandering in a daze on a Nebraska highway. Initially it was thought she was the victim of a hit-and-run accident. Later it was learned that the young woman had wounds which could have resulted from injury prior to the accident and that on the afternoon of her death she had been picked up from her father's home by a dark-haired man driving a car matching the description of one often used by Douglass Durham.

AIM's investigation of Durham also led to a re-examination of the bizarre case of Paul Durant Skyhorse, a Minnesota Chippewa, and Richard Billings Mohawk, a Tuscarora/Mohawk from the Niagara Falls area. These two AIM organizers had been active in Chicago and on the West Coast and in October 1974, were staying at AIM's Camp 13 in Box Canyon, about 90 miles north of Los Angeles. Some of the camp's costs had been paid by Los Angeles businessman George Roberts. Its entrance bore the sign "Centre of Spirituality", but whatever its original purpose, the camp had become a crash pad where drugs and alcohol were often used heavily.

On October 10, 1974, five persons staying at the camp went to the Hollywood Hills home of television actor David Carradine and had a party in his absence. Three of them—Holly Broussard, her boyfriend, Marvin Red Shirt, and Marcia Eaglestaff McNoise—called for a taxi to take them back to the Box Canyon Camp. Before the evening was over, George Aird, the 26-year-old cab driver who responded to the call, was brutally stabbed and his body stuffed into a dry well at the camp.

Initially Broussard, Red Shirt and McNoise were charged with the murder. There appeared to be much circumstantial evidence implicating them: blood stains on pants and boots they wore, blood on a book and knife belonging to Holly Broussard, and other evidence. Subsequently they were granted immunity from prosecution in exchange for testimony implicating Skyhorse and Mohawk in the murder. Evidence uncovered by Skyhorse and Mohawk's defence suggests that Los Angeles area police had some pre-existing plan to raid the camp. Several days before the murder, Douglass Durham had visited Camp 13 and questioned Paul Skyhorse extensively about his plans. Skyhorse indicated that he intended to go to an Indian education conference in Phoenix, Arizona, which is where he was later arrested. When the two AIM members were charged with killing George Aird, Durham recommended that AIM repudiate them and support instead the three who were given immunity. For nearly two years, while awaiting trial, Skyhorse and Mohawk were abandoned by AIM, held in solitary confinement and harassed by prison guards.

Durham's full role in the case remains unclear. He approached a long-time AIM member shortly before the murder, attempting to convince him to take charge of the Box Canyon camp and speaking of "big plans" for an incident which would "expose the racism of the sheriff's department and all those people in the area". Despite the evidence of Durham's involvement, and that of at least one other FBI operative, the presiding judge in the Skyhorse-Mohawk trial refused to order that FBI files on the case be disclosed to the defence. Following Durham's exposure as an FBI spy, AIM belatedly began to support the two defendants.

In the winter of 1975-76, following his exposure as an FBI operative, Douglass Durham, minus his Indian identity, lectured throughout the midwestern states on a tour sponsored by the John Birch Society. He told stories of AIM's "communist" links, its alleged propensity to violence and its affiliations with terrorist organizations. Durham told the same story to the Senate Subcommittee on Internal Security in April 1976. The committee, headed by Senator James Eastland of Mississippi, staged a major press conference in Washington, D.C. in September 1976, six months after Durham had testified, to announce the slanderous allegations to the nation. Eastland chose to call no other witnesses before releasing the report and heard testimony from no native Americans, but concluded flatly that "AIM does not speak for American Indians".

Durham's allegations, as reported by the committee, received widespread press coverage. One committee member, Senator Birch Bayh, refused to take part in the proceedings and condemned the internal security subcommittee for issuing a report "on the basis of the unchallenged testimony of one solitary witness". Bayh called the findings "totally unacceptable" and concluded that the hearing and the report "seem to have no other purpose than to discredit a number of individuals, including...the American Indian Movement". Durham's testimony before the Eastland committee may have been his last active attempt to damage AIM and was perhaps the least effective, for the exposure of his two years of spying within the organization had already left AIM with a legacy of fear, mistrust and suspicion which was as crippling as any specific acts of disruption.

7/The Making of a Warrior

By the time Douglass Durham was exposed as an FBI agent in early 1975, Anna Mae Aquash had become a widely respected member of the American Indian Movement. She counted among her friends a number of AIM's national leaders and was approaching the level of a national decision-maker in her own right. Following the occupation of Wounded Knee in 1973 the American Indian Movement became the focus of her life.

Anna Mae's divorce from Jake Maloney in mid-1970 had left her with custody of the couple's two children. Almost immediately after the divorce, Maloney married the young, white secretary at the Matson karate studio in Boston. He sold his interest in the business and used the proceeds to establish his own karate school in Halifax. More than ever he was "Mr. Karate", giving demonstrations on the Nova Scotia reserves and winning widespread admiration for his financial success. While Anna Mae was in Wounded Knee in 1973, Maloney removed their daughters Denise and Deborah from the care of Mary Lafford and took them back to Halifax. Though legal custody remained with Anna Mae, she agreed to let the children stay with their father for the summer, while she and her second husband, Nogeeshik Aquash decided where they would make their home.

The veterans of the Wounded Knee occupation were shocked to discover that beyond Pine Ridge Reservation, values, opinions and concerns had changed very little. For two months the occupiers of the village had lived in a war-like atmosphere, their nerves taut, their attention narrowed to the basics—defence, food, shelter and negotiations with the U.S. government. They had created a close-knit community based on Indian spirituality and Indian values, a community unified by adversity, where there was pride, not shame, in being Indian. On May 8, 1973 that community vanished. The occupiers walked out into a world that for the most part viewed their action not as an heroic struggle for a just cause but as reprehensible hooliganism. To the FBI they were terrorists and subversives. While the participants in the 71-day occupation felt as if they had aged several years, the world outside continued as before.

After Wounded Knee, Anna Mae and Nogeeshik Aquash experimented with several ideas. They returned to Boston intending to start an AIM survival school where Indian children failing in the white school system could learn in an Indian atmosphere. They could not arrange funding for the project and abandoned the idea. They went to Nogeeshik's home reserve on Walpole Island in Lake St. Clair with thoughts of building their own home there, but that plan did not work out either. In the early fall, Anna Mae asked her young daughters to decide which parent they wanted to live with, and the children chose to remain with Jake Maloney and his wife in Halifax. Anna Mae respected the decision but it grieved her deeply. She wanted her daughters brought up in an Indian community and felt that Jake Maloney and his new wife had won the children's affection by giving them things that she could not afford.

In the fall of 1973, Anna Mae and Nogeeshik settled in Ottawa, where they began to organize a show of fashions, beadwork and jewellery based on traditional Indian designs. She took a temporary job as director of a youth drop-in centre to support herself and to earn money to buy materials for her own contributions to the fashion show. The exhibit was eventually staged at Ottawa's National Arts Centre in May 1974 and received wide acclaim.

As would be the case everywhere she travelled, Anna Mae made good friends in Ottawa. "If she liked you she was like a sister to you," said one woman who enjoyed Anna Mae's sense of humour and found her "really gentle". The same friend noted

Anna Mae's determination and the stubborn way in which she clung to her opinions. Anna Mae was not quick to jump to conclusions, but when she made up her mind it was almost impossible to shake her beliefs. At the same time she had developed the tough, cool side of her personality which appeared as confidence and the ability to handle herself well in public. She began more and more to hide the vulnerable aspects of her character which sometimes left her feeling lonely and dependent.

Anna Mae told some friends she wanted to avoid drawing attention to herself, but she and Nogeeshik soon let themselves be drawn into a social life revolving around the pubs frequented by the increasing number of Indians in Ottawa. Nogeeshik tended to become involved in scraps when he drank, and Anna Mae herself showed an abrasive side under the influence of alcohol. On one occasion, she embarrassed her companions by launching a uncontrolled tirade against the Indian director of a northwestern Ontario Indian residential school. The institution had gained notoriety when Charlie Wenjack, a 12-year-old pupil, froze to death while trying to run away from the school and return to his family. Anna Mae accused the director of being a traitor to his race and, pointing at his crippled arm, demanded shrilly, "Did you get that in punishment?"

Incidents such as this marred her efforts to "lie low"; but she rarely spoke publicly of her involvement in the Wounded Knee occupation, saving stories about it for the few individuals she knew she could trust not to divulge them. "It was just like a movie," one friend later said of Anna Mae's vivid description of the siege. During recurring spells of depression she confided to her friend her sense of foreboding, saying she was sure she didn't have long to live and that she would be "executed". In response to admonitions not to be foolish, Anna Mae replied, "No, it's true. That's what they do to Indians who fight for their people."

By the end of 1973, according to friends, Anna Mae and Nogeeshik's marriage, sanctified in Wounded Knee, was foundering. He was often attracted to white women and sometimes used them to taunt his wife. She would respond with a cutting barb, but it seemed she still depended on him emotionally and was distressed by the prospect of another break-up. There was little permanence in her life and some friends thought she missed the feeling of belonging to a community. Some thought that Nogeeshik provided her with a kind of stability and that she admired his dedication to his Indian identity. But he also confused her, belying his convictions when he drank and failing to match her determination and strength of will. The couple's quarrels grew more frequent and violent, and they separated several times.

In early 1974, Anna Mae went to St. Paul, and throughout that spring she divided her time between Minnesota and Ottawa, finally making St. Paul her base after the successful completion of the Arts Centre fashion show in Ottawa in May. She and Nogeeshik, who turned up there later, were among thousands of Indian people who flocked to the Minnesota capital during the eight-month trial of Dennis Banks and Russell Means. Even those Indians who did not consider Banks and Means their spokesmen regarded the trial as a vehicle for the airing of grievances that had been ignored for many years. Many who could not attend sent letters of support and contributed to the defence fund.

In AIM's national office in St. Paul, Anna Mae contributed her considerable energies and ideas. Shortly after arriving in St. Paul she suggested a project that she hoped would make AIM less dependent on the financial support of church groups. She had researched the history of ribbon shirts in her efforts to learn about the history of the Micmac tribe. She believed that these shirts originated with a band of Micmacs who in time of need had accepted cassocks from a small monastery and decorated them with buttons, military braid, ribbons and anything they could find to relieve the drab ugliness of the garments. Eventually, certain decorations came to signify specific deeds. Anna Mae proposed to organize the women who had flocked to the trial, many of whom could not get into the small spectator gallery, to sew ribbon shirts which would then be sold to Minneapolis-St. Paul shops. She and others sought donations of cloth and ribbon and enlisted the help of about 50 women who set to work on the sewing. Anna Mae wrote a short leaflet so that the purchaser would get not only a piece of clothing but a small piece of Indian history as well. The fund-raising plan collapsed, however, when the garments proved so popular with boyfriends and husbands that they were given away and there were none left to sell.

Personal fitness was important to Anna Mae; she believed that as an Indian fighter she needed physical strength as well as mental ability. She swam and jogged and was one of the few women to take part in karate practices in the AIM house gymnasium. She'd become proficient in the sport through her workouts with Jake Maloney. Her skill was said to equal that of a brown-belt; at any rate she was able to outmanoeuvre some of the men, including Nogeeshik.

Tension increased in the couple's on-again, off-again marriage until, following an afternoon in the pub, Anna Mae took a .357-calibre handgun and threatened to commit suicide, shooting two bullets into the dashboard of Nogeeshik's car. Returning to the apartment she shared with other AIM members she staged another melodramatic scene, splattering herself with ketchup and leaving behind a ketchup-stained knife in the bathroom. It was clearly an appeal for sympathy. "She always liked, and was good at, dramatics," said one observer. Friends said her relationship with Nogeeshik had deteriorated badly and that the resulting tension took a heavy toll on the young woman. The sometimes frantic, emotion-charged trial atmosphere did little to provide relief from these personal problems.

Anna Mae had also begun, in the summer of 1974, an intimate relationship with AIM leader Dennis Banks, whose young wife, Kamook, she had counted among her friends. According to some, the affair meant much more to Anna Mae than it did to Banks. She was said to be just one of several intelligent, capable women who worked for Banks and developed a strong, emotional attachment for him. By the late fall of 1974, Anna Mae had become known as Dennis' West Coast woman, a label she disliked but which described the reality of the relationship. It continued to pose a serious dilemma for her because she knew she was betraying her friend Kamook. She told friends that she wanted some time "to talk to Kamook about Dennis" but did not do so, an omission which later had serious consequences.

Anna Mae's mock-suicide attempt was followed closely by her permanent separation from Nogeeshik. This relieved some of the emotional tension in her life and left her feeling happier and freer. While the separation seemed to be good for her it was an act which "violated the pipe"—the dictates of the traditional ceremony by which she and Nogeeshik had been married—and thus caused Anna Mae to feel there was impending doom in her life. Because she had had to discover old spiritual ways for herself, after she reached adulthood, she valued them highly and violation of them was a serious matter for her. Within AIM she became known as a strongly spiritual person who studied with traditional spiritual leaders whenever possible. She took part regularly in the cleansing and purifying ceremonies of the sweat lodge and was preparing herself in 1974 to take part in the Sioux Sundance by praying at dusk and at dawn.

For activists like Anna Mae Aquash, the traditional ceremonies were a powerful motivating force. Her ancestors had been among the earliest converts to Christianity, and many of the Micmac ways had fallen into disuse; but she had researched the available sources for knowledge of her own tribe's past and had participated in the spiritual ceremonies of other tribes. She saw the traditional religion as a way of unifying Indian people, a way of recreating a focal point to give meaning to their lives and make possible collective action and struggle.

During this time in her life, Anna Mae spent a short time at occupied Anicinabe Park in Kenora, Ontario. She hitch-hiked from St. Paul and swam across a bay in the Lake of the Woods to gain entry, barely escaping police detection. She then travelled from Kenora to Nova Scotia to visit her daughters. As she was returning the two little girls to Jake Maloney's suburban home, one of them told her, "Mommy, you know what? We'll never forget you Mommy." After leaving the Maloney home she discovered a wad of papers stuffed into her jacket pocket. They were legal documents notifying her that Jake had finally adopted the girls, thereby gaining exclusive legal custody. She was enraged by the deed and the underhanded manner in which it had been carried out.

Because Anna Mae and Jake were not married when the daughters were born, he was forced to go through formal adoption procedures to become a legal parent. The girls had been living with him because Anna Mae consented to abide by the children's wishes. Now that he had adopted them, it was clear that if she wanted to regain custody she would have a legal battle on her hands—it was no longer a matter of a friendly arrangement. To avoid losing her daughters permanently she would have to give up her unsettled lifestyle and her work with AIM and return to Nova Scotia. Even then she might not be successful. She was confronted with a choice which she was not ready to make.

During this same visit, Anna Mae told friends in Nova Scotia to watch the newspapers for the outcome of the Banks-Means trial. Banks had considered going into exile if he were convicted, she said, and if he did she would go with him. This plan was never tested. "We were relieved when they got off," said one friend, "because it meant we would have her with us a little longer."

In St. Paul, Anna Mae continued her work in the AIM office and also spent time at the Red Schoolhouse teaching Indian students how to do research and make effective use of libraries. This activity was part of a long-cherished project she had frequently discussed with others, aimed at creating "true reservation histories" for tribes across Canada and the United States. Much of that history existed in the oral tradition of the elders on the reservations; but Anna Mae argued that simply recording their stories was not enough. No matter how little disruption there had been in a tribe, the elders would have forgotten a great deal, and she hoped that AIM survival schools would train students to do the library research that ought to accompany such a project. Her goal was that eventually there would be several hundred Indian people trained to do this work.

Anna Mae discussed with Paula Giese, a former humanities professor at the University of Minnesota, the problems involved in this kind of cultural research. Translation into English and transposition from oral legend to print had robbed Indian legends of their meaning. Many had been diluted by prim Victorian anthropologists who had stripped the stories of their sexual content and diminished them to the level of whimsical fairy tales. Giese recalls being impressed by Anna Mae's intellectual abilities and thought "she had a well-stocked mind. It was clear she had thought and read a lot." It was an opinion shared by others who came to know Anna Mae, although perhaps no one was as effusive as her own sister, Mary Lafford, who marvelled at "the ideas she used to come out with. She could think like nobody else!"

Anna Mae had little use for ivory tower scholarship, and she always sought to apply her ideas directly to the life she was living. She was among a handful of AIM members concerned with planning the long-range programs they believed the organization should be developing. "She could see a hundred years from now," said Paula Giese, "and she could see what had to be done to get from here to there." This strategic and intellectual bent, which had also characterized many of her discussions with friends during the Wounded Knee occupation, was uncommon in AIM and even rarer among women in its male-dominated structure. Anna Mae did not allow it to set her apart from others, however, and she continued to be able to befriend individuals of varying backgrounds and of all ages. In this respect, her childhood ability to put herself in the place of others continued to serve her well. In some cases, though, it had unforeseen consequences: Mary Lafford believes that Anna Mae almost unconsciously mimicked those she was with. Within a short time of meeting people she could be talking like them and adopting their mannerisms. This quality, according to Lafford, accounted for some of Anna Mae's personal difficulties: "After a while she showed men themselves and they didn't like it."

In the fall of 1974, Anna Mae, well-established in AIM, took on increasing responsibilities. She became one of a small group—including Darelle "Dino" Butler—who reorganized the Los Angeles chapter of AIM into a highly effective fund-raising operation. Part of her work included contacting affluent liberals and show business personalities and enlisting their financial support for AIM. By some accounts her efforts were undermined by Douglass Durham who persuaded some supporters to entrust to him funds that had been promised Anna Mae. In late 1974 Durham had become such a disruptive influence in the Los Angeles chapter that one day an angry Anna Mae called St. Paul. "I want a national leader out here and I want him on the next plane," she demanded. It was only after help arrived that she learned that Durham had been sent out deliberately by St. Paul AIM to give some of its members a chance to check out their suspicions that Durham was an FBI agent.

Anna Mae's rising stature within AIM was demonstrated further during the Menominee Warrior Society occupation of the Gresham novitiate in January 1975, when she was assigned to provide security for the radio set in the Keshena, Wisconsin support base. She wore the gun she had been given in a shoulder holster which reached almost down to her waist, as if it were a pendant of rare design which she wore with swaggering pride, but with the knowledge that it represented authority. After Douglass Durham left the scene of the occupation, Anna Mae and others assumed responsibility for media relations.

When Dennis Banks told her their relationship was to end she wrote a poem expressing her sadness:

But the sun is up and you're going?
My heart is filled with tears
please don't go, I need you walking by my side...
The road is long and weary
And I get so tired...

The reasons for the break-up were political as well as personal. Banks' marriage to the young Oglala Sioux woman, Kamook, established for him an important political link with the Pine Ridge Reservation, which was a key base of AIM support and operations. Anna Mae knew, therefore, that her relationship with Banks could never be anything more than a casual one. Nevertheless, she wished it could be different and confided to friends she was disappointed not to be able to fill the role she dreamt of—as Banks' lieutenant in a continuing struggle on behalf of Indian people.

Following the disastrous Menominee occupation, Anna Mae

returned to St. Paul to help organize a benefit concert for the AIM survival schools—the Red Schoolhouse in St. Paul, the Heart of the Earth School in Minneapolis, and the We Will Remember School in Rapid City, South Dakota. Singers Harry Belafonte, Kris Kristofferson, Rita Coolidge and Buffy St. Marie were among the entertainers at the standing-room-only event. Anna Mae's backstage efforts were typical of the way she worked, avoiding the limelight but making sure essential things were done.

By the spring of 1975 she was recognized and respected as an organizer in her own right and was taking an increasing role in the decision-making of AIM policies and programs. When she believed in an idea—such as the need for solid ongoing programs to back up the dramatic confrontations that had become AIM's trademark—she pushed them aggressively and relentlessly. She was concerned about the AIM education programs that were being pursued in the survival schools. These schools were among the most positive achievements of the movement. They took in Indian youngsters who had dropped out of the public school system and gave them an Indian education, helping many achieve a degree of academic success that would otherwise have been unavailable to them. Anna Mae argued that an added dimension was also needed—programs which would train AIM leaders so that the movement would not depend on a handful of vulnerable leaders. She believed new leaders should be continually emerging, regenerating AIM's momentum, strengthening the movement and broadening its appeal. It was a vision that seemed remote to most of the AIM leaders, who were preoccupied with the problems of short-term survival. More than half the Wounded Knee cases were still to come to trial, and the movement was reeling from the public exposure of FBI operative Douglass Durham.

At about the same time, residents of the Pine Ridge Reservation were paying a high price for AIM's limited victories and for their own rebellion at Wounded Knee. Violence on the reservation reached unprecedented heights in the two years after the occupation. There were 23 murders in 1974 alone, giving the reservation a higher murder rate than the city of Chicago. During the 1975 reign of terror, attacks on AIM members and their supporters increased further, finally prompting the Department of the Interior—the parent body of the BIA—to set up a commission of inquiry into reservation lawlessness.

It was an attack on AIM lawyers and legal workers in February 1975 that precipitated the establishment of the commission. The group had flown to the reservation to tour key areas in preparation for the defence of AIM clients. Upon their return to the Pine Ridge airstrip they were confronted by Richard Wilson and a dozen goons who assaulted them, stabbing one woman with a knife. Their car was demolished and their airplane riddled with bullets. The incident was unusual only in that it involved whites.

In all, in the first six months of 1975, there were 18 murders and 67 attacks on persons and property on the reservation. In February 1975, veteran BIA police officer Jess Trueblood walked up to the Pine Ridge home of Bernice Stone and sprayed it with rifle fire, sending Mrs. Stone and four others to hospital. Later Trueblood's body was found, a rifle bullet in the back of his head. In March, the home of respected Oglala Sioux chief Frank Fools Crow was shot up. The trailer home of AIM supporter Poker Joe Merrivale was likewise peppered, one bullet striking the mattress where he lay sleeping. On March 9, 1975, AIM supporter Jeanette Bissonnette was driving home from the wake of a friend who had been murdered when she was killed by a bullet shot through the back of her light blue station wagon from another car.

In most cases the victims of the violence were AIM members and supporters. The perpetrators were seldom arrested, or if arrested, rarely convicted. During the 1973 occupation of Wounded Knee, Richard Wilson and his goons had set up their own roadblocks and on one occasion stopped the Chief United States Marshal and the Assistant U.S. Attorney General and pointed a rifle at the latter's head. The FBI broke up the confrontation but no charges were laid. Following the 1975 attack on the AIM attorneys, Richard Wilson again received preferential treatment. A desultory investigation by the FBI resulted in a federal grand jury bringing misdemeanor charges against Wilson. An all-white jury acquitted him. Later Wilson admitted he had ordered the beating of the "agitators" and said it was a "justifiable stomping".

The situation on Pine Ridge took on yet another dimension when, during the early months of 1975, a number of AIM supporters took up residence on the reservation. Dennis Banks, who was still facing riot charges arising from the Custer, South Dakota confrontation two years earlier, moved into a tiny cabin near the residence of Harry and Cecilia Jumping Bull, three miles east of the settlement of Oglala. Banks lived there with his wife and daughter while on trial in Custer.

Oglala residents had seen their share of violence and had come to expect an absence of police protection. One Oglala family, for example, returned from a Nebraska shopping trip to find their house stripped of its contents—thieves had even taken the food from the refrigerator. No BIA police responded to the family's repeated pleas for help. Finally they appealed to AIM members who issued a warning and demanded that the goods be returned within 24 hours. Early next morning, the family was led to a ditch where their belongings had been stashed.

But in other incidents AIM members and their supporters were the objects of brutal attacks. Despite the increased number of lawmen on the reservation to stem the growing violence, Oglala residents were virtually without police protection. In one such attack, Dorothy Brings 'Em Back was beaten into unconsciousness and shot at by her assailants. The high-velocity bullets came within inches of her body, causing it to flip over in the air. Her attackers fled, assuming wrongly that she was dead. No one was charged with the assault which left Brings 'Em Back with broken ribs and other injuries. She alleges that her assailants were goons employed by then tribal chairman Richard Wilson.

By the end of May more AIM members, returning from the organization's annual convention in Farmington, New Mexico, moved onto the reservation. Many lived on the Jumping Bull land in an encampment that came to be known as "Tent City". They gradually assumed a role as defenders of the Oglala community.

Among those who came to the reservation that spring was Anna Mae Aquash. She lived for some time in a small trailer located about half way between Oglala and the Jumping Bull place. Her organizing efforts were directed mainly at the Oglala women, who did not always respond well to the initiatives of male leaders. Anna Mae took part in their quilting bees and in the rummage sales they held to raise money. Her sewing and beadwork skills were much admired and she quickly befriended a number of Oglala women. She often led their discussions beyond the usual small talk to the topic of Sioux treaty rights, the land they had lost and the poor living conditions on the reservation. She pointed out the nutritional inadequacy of the food they were given under the commodity program, which provided them with quantities of lard, flour, dried and canned foods. "I wouldn't feed that canned meat to my dog," she said on one occasion. "You're so brainwashed you just let everything go. That's how come you end up like this."

Anna Mae roused the other women's anger, indignation and fighting spirit. She was able to reach the women and move them to fight against the hardships of reservation life in a way the male leaders of AIM were not able to do. The women knew that Anna Mae had experienced hardships similar to their own and that she now shared their life. She often spoke about her daughters and the pain she felt being separated from them. She told of her poverty-stricken childhood and of how, when some financial security had been hers, it had not proven to be enough. "After I realized how you people live, I didn't want the things I had before," she told Roslyn Jumping Bull. "I left everything because I wanted to show you I love you people and want to help you."

Anna Mae had already found it necessary to adopt an alias, and she was introduced to Oglala people as Joanna Jason. There were some indications that she had already been targeted by the FBI. Agent David Price used the murder of Jeanette Bissonnette as a pretext to detain and interrogate her—by then a common FBI tactic. The practice was doubly useful: the agents might pry information from their subject and in addition the very fact of the interrogation served to raise doubts among associates. Had the person succumbed to FBI threats, given information, been persuaded to cooperate in FBI plans?

Rumours of informers and suspected informers were widespread in the American Indian Movement, according to some observers. Personal animosities and jealousies, factional rivalry or leadership struggles—which the FBI often sought to heighten—led to idle accusations that an individual was "a pig", and the loose talk was seldom controlled.

In Anna Mae's case it did not take long for such rumours to surface. At the end of May, within a month of her interrogation, Anna Mae arrived at the national AIM convention in Farmington, New Mexico only to learn that her relationship with Dennis Banks had been revealed to his wife Kamook, who was predictably resentful. The anger and envy helped fan rumours that Anna Mae Aquash was an informer for the FBI. She left the convention "confused and mixed up" and spoke of going back home to Nova Scotia to fight for custody of her children and work for the Micmac tribe.

However, she returned to Pine Ridge to continue her work there. One of her goals was to organize the women to demand improvements in the commodities program because she believed that the commodities failed to provide adequate nutrition. She felt that dietary deficiencies contributed largely to the apathy, listlessness and susceptibility to illness and alcoholism prevalent among reservation residents. She also worked to support the legal defence of AIM leaders Stan Holder, Carter Camp and Leonard Crow Dog, the Sioux spiritual leader, who all still faced felony charges stemming from the Wounded Knee occupation. Although her reputation had been somewhat undermined by rumours, Anna Mae continued at least for a while to work effectively on the reservation.

8/Fugitives

Tension mounted throughout May and June 1975 as AIM members continued their efforts to protect Oglala residents against goon attacks and advise them of their rights under U.S. law and under the 1868 Fort Laramie treaty. On June 26, their low-key grassroots political work suffered a dramatic setback.

On the morning of June 26, FBI agents Ray Williams and Jack Coler visited a number of homes in the Oglala area looking for Jimmy Eagle. Eagle had allegedly been one of a group involved in a late-night drinking brawl on June 23, in which Indian youths detained two white farm hands, then released them unharmed but minus a pair of cowboy boots. As a result, Eagle and three others were charged with kidnapping.

When the two agents came to the Jumping Bull compound—where Dennis Banks was living while on trial in Custer, South Dakota—they were told that Eagle did not live or visit there. When Wallace "June" Little Jr., who lived near the Jumping Bulls, asked the agents what right they had to trespass on private land, he was shown a list of four names, individuals he knew lived in other parts of the reservation. The agents said they had arrest warrants for the four, including Jimmy Eagle, but no arrest warrants were shown.

The agents returned to the Jumping Bull property shortly before noon. Within minutes a gun battle broke out. When it was over, six hours later, the two FBI men and an Indian, 24-year-old Joe Stuntz, were dead. Scores of federal agents surrounded the property and the Jumping Bull house was riddled with bullets, tear-gassed and its interior ransacked by the FBI. What precipitated the shoot-out, or who was responsible for the initial shots, remains unclear to this day, despite evidence given in two related trials.

The initial version of events as described by the FBI, however, seemed designed to obfuscate rather than clarify what had transpired that day. The Bureau first claimed that the two officers had been ambushed while trying to serve an arrest warrant on the four persons charged with kidnapping in the cowboy boot incident. Later they said they meant that one of the four, Jimmy Eagle, was sought at what became the site of the gunbattle. The two agents had driven to "June" Little's house in one car and had found themselves in the midst of an area well fortified with trenches and bunkers, from which the attack came. Each agent had been shot 20 to 25 times, official statements said, and had been dragged from the car. The dead Indian, Joe Stuntz, was wearing the jacket of one of the dead agents, according to this version. Stuntz had been shot in the forehead during the exchange of gunfire. These reports claimed that AIM leaders had planned the ambush. They had been wanting to "get" an FBI agent, said one news report, quoting official sources. The slain FBI men just had time to radio for help before they died. Sixteen Indian men and eight women who had engaged in the gunbattle with police escaped through the police lines encircling the Jumping Bull land.

In the days and weeks that followed, this initial FBI scenario underwent considerable revision. News reporters arriving on the scene immediately after the shoot-out noted that Joe Stuntz had not been shot in the forehead: the slain Indian man was lying on his back and blood seemed to be coming from underneath the jacket he was wearing, down the arms and wrists. Reporters noted that the three-room Jumping Bull house was full of bullet holes, particularly the stucco additions to the log house, but they saw no bunkers or trenches, only dilapidated root cellars where the Jumping Bulls had stored food.

A statement by FBI Director Clarence Kelley released a few days after the shootings revealed that each of the two FBI men had been shot only three times and one had been shot in the foot and the hand as well as the head. This cast doubt on the execution story the Bureau had previously put forth. The FBI's initial claims were contradicted further when, on July 9, the *Washington Post* revealed that state Attorney General William Janklow had admitted that state troopers had been monitoring and taping FBI transmissions and that these tapes showed the dead agents had been in two cars, radioing messages back and forth. When the shooting started, they had been chasing a red pick-up truck that officials said matched the vehicle wanted in the so-called kidnapping case. One of the agent's cars was found to the northwest of the Jumping Bulls' near the spot where the bodies were located. The other was found some distance to the east, overlooking AIM's Tent City.

Occupants of the Tent City fled the area on foot, hiding in culverts and woods to avoid detection. Witnesses say federal agents and some of Richard Wilson's goon squad saw them leave the Jumping Bull land and fired numerous shots which missed the mark. They did not give chase, however. Oglala residents noted that large numbers of BIA and FBI agents—far exceeding the normal contingent on the reservation—responded within an hour of Coler and William's call for help. By nightfall—and for the next two weeks—there were close to 200 agents on the reservation. Some Indian people charged that the FBI had planned an attack on the AIM encampment but that the plan had backfired causing the death of the two agents. AIM charged that the shooting of Joe Stuntz by the agents prompted Indian people in the area to return fire. Neither claim has been proved.

When the four Indians sought in the cowboy boot incident were finally taken into custody they were charged not with kidnapping but with robbery and assault. One of the four, Jimmy Eagle, surrendered on his own. Much later he was also charged with the murder of the two FBI agents, even though witnesses said he was in Pine Ridge village during the shoot-out. The charges against Eagle were dropped several months later.

Immediately after the gunbattle, between 150 and 200 FBI agents, including a Special Weapons and Tactics (SWAT) Team, began to comb the Pine Ridge Reservation. The agents were dressed in military fatigues, carried high-powered M-16 automatic weapons and were equipped with helicopters, airplanes, jeeps and dogs. Two years after the Wounded Knee occupation, armoured personnel carriers again became a familiar sight on the reservation. For days following the shoot-out, reservation roads were blockaded and Pine Ridge was in a state of siege. In effect, the FBI had declared martial law on its own authority.

Many residents of the White Clay district, the area in which Oglala is situated, asserted their treaty rights by signing a petition which demanded the "removal of all alien law enforcement personnel—the South Dakota Highway Patrol, the U.S. Marshals, the Special Weapons and Tactical Team, the FBI and the U.S. Army from our district". Complaints from reservation residents about multiple violations of their civil rights prompted an investigation by the United States Commission on Civil Rights, an independent body that reports directly to Congress. Commission investigator William Muldrow wrote in a July 9 memo to his superiors that he received many complaints of "threats, harassment and search procedures conducted without due process of law by the FBI". Residents said FBI agents threatened them, made contemptuous, racist remarks and tried to buy information. Muldrow noted that many Indian people were deeply resentful of the FBI's invasion of the reservation, "a procedure that would [not] be tolerated in any non-Indian community in the United States". He questioned the basis of the FBI's jurisdiction on the reservation, noted the overlap with BIA functions and asked if it were proper that the Bureau, which had furnished adversary witnesses for the Wounded Knee trials, should now be acting as the investigatory agency.

The U.S. Justice Department, however, did not respond to the letter it received from the Civil Rights Commission detailing these concerns; nor did authorities respond to the petition of the White Clay residents or the injunctions requested by WKLDOC attorneys who sought the removal of the massive FBI force on the grounds that the civil rights of Pine Ridge residents were being systematically violated. Legal formalities were ignored as FBI agents, acting in cooperation with the BIA police, arrested persons solely to obtain information and to remove them from circulation, WKLDOC attorneys charged. The attorneys also charged that agents photographed and questioned individuals, deceived them into signing waivers of their rights and forced them to take lie detector tests.

The FBI, however, denied that it was doing anything other than carrying out its duties "in the best possible way". A Bureau spokesman admitted to one search without a warrant but claimed the Indian property owner had given permission voluntarily. The victim said that two helicopters of combat-ready agents had landed unexpectedly in his yard and approached his house pointing automatic weapons. "What do you mean 'gave permission'?" he asked later. "When they came running at us with rifles pointed, we didn't say *anything*."

Five months after the shootings, a federal grand jury handed down murder indictments in the slaying of the agents. Charged were AIM leader Leonard Peltier, Robert Robideau and Darelle "Dino" Butler. Joe Stuntz's death was never investigated. Officials continue to say that he "got caught in the cross-fire". In the meantime the FBI investigation on the Pine Ridge Reservation continued in the manner of a search and destroy mission.

The Bureau seems to have decided very early in the investigation whom it wanted in connection with the killings and had asked Canadian officials for help in the search. Early in July—within days of the shootings—RCMP officials in Ottawa opened files on the suspects. Included in the list of those wanted for questioning was Anna Mae Pictou Aquash. RCMP officers were asked to question her family concerning her whereabouts.

Anna Mae Aquash had not been on the Jumping Bull land on June 26; she had been in Cedar Rapids, Iowa, where AIM leaders Stan Holder, Carter Camp and Leonard Crow Dog had been on trial and convicted. She had addressed a citizens' group on behalf of the Indian leaders, speaking particularly of the unjust charge against the well-known Sioux spiritual leader Crow Dog. But as the FBI agents combed the reservation, they persisted in asking about Anna Mae Aquash, or Anna Mae Pictou, where she had been and why she had left. In fact, Anna Mae remained on the reservation all that summer but managed to evade detection.

One day in August, Anna Mae was visiting the WKLDOC legal workers in Oglala when FBI agents arrived. Fearing that they might come crashing in, with or without a warrant, Anna Mae hid in a tiny crawl-space in the rafters of the one-room cabin. As a young mother in Boston she had hidden in a refrigerator while playing hide-and-seek; this time it was no game. She wanted no contact with the FBI, because it was dangerous to be even in the position of having to refuse to talk to them. When it became clear that the agents outside were going to stay for some time, she emerged from her hiding place, coolly slipped into the front seat of a car between two Indian men and drove right past the agents, arousing no suspicion.

Anna Mae had compelling reasons to avoid contact with the FBI. At the end of July, she, Dennis Banks and a group of Oglala women drove together from Oglala to Crow Dog's Paradise on the Rosebud Reservation, which abuts the eastern border of Pine Ridge, to attend the annual Sioux Sundance. There, according to one report, she quarrelled with Leonard Crow Dog who wanted an account of the conversations that had taken place en route. Crow Dog and others, including Anna Mae's close friend Leonard Peltier, accused her of being an FBI spy and told her to leave the Sundance grounds. Shaken and in tears, she returned to Pine Ridge, determined to clear her name. By then, mistrust among AIM members was at an all-time high, fanned by the Durham spy disclosures, by the tensions and hardships that followed the June 26 shoot-out and by the FBI's pursuit of AIM leaders. At a Montana gathering on July 18, AIM leader Vernon Bellecourt brought Bernie Morning Gun to the platform and told the assembled crowd that Morning Gun had been an FBI informer for two years. On this occasion, Bellecourt announced a 30-day amnesty for all self-confessed informers, except for those whose work had included attempts on the lives of AIM leaders.

Discussing the rumours about herself with friends, Anna Mae had said, "These Indians better stop talking like that. Soon they'll be shooting each other for no reason." Accusations of this sort had caused a gunfight betwen AIM leaders Carter Camp and Clyde Bellecourt in the summer of 1973.

Throughout the summer and fall, the FBI continued its manhunt for the three suspected murderers. The fact that two of their own colleagues had been killed gave the actions of some of the agents the desperate and determined air of a vendetta. By August, the FBI alert to Ottawa RCMP headquarters had been transmitted to the RCMP office in Truro, Nova Scotia, but it was September 9 before Corporal Wayne MacNeill of the Antigonish detachment went out to the nearby Afton Reserve to speak to Anna Mae's brother-in-law, Earl Lafford. By then the FBI had successfully stalked their quarry.

On the morning of September 5, residents and guests at Al Running's place on the Rosebud Reservation woke up to shouts of "We're the FBI. Come out or we'll shoot." Nearly 50 FBI men dressed in bullet-proof vests and combat fatigues and carrying M-16 automatic rifles poured out of cars at the front of the Running residence. The FBI claims the raid involved a total of 50 men, but eyewitnesses say more federal agents emerged from the surrounding bush and still others came by canoe up the stream behind the house. Helicopters circled overhead and the early morning half-light was hazy from the explosion of a half-dozen smoke bombs. A similar raid was taking place about a mile down the road at the home of Running's brother-in-law, Leonard Crow Dog.

The pretext for the pre-dawn invasion was the FBI's intention to serve arrest warrants on five men who had been involved in a minor scuffle two days before. On September 2, Al Running had gone to a spot north of Pine Ridge village, 90 miles west of his home, to pick up his 17-year-old son who had been beaten by two men. The following day he met the pair at the Crow Dog place, bragging about the assault. The ensuing fight was soon broken up but resulted in warrants for the arrest of Running, Crow Dog and three others, warrants which the FBI chose to serve before dawn on September 5.

The massive raid was typical of the way the FBI searched for the suspected murderers of the two agents throughout the summer and early fall of 1975. Moreover, rumours circulating on the

Rosebud reservation pinpointed the Running and Crow Dog residences as hideouts for fugitives. Among those staying with Running were Anna Mae Aquash, Darelle "Dino" Butler and his wife Nilak. None had charges outstanding against them, but on the morning of September 5, both Butler and Anna Mae were immediately arrested.

Anna Mae later described these events in a taped interview with WKLDOC workers. She awoke to voices outside her tent saying, "Let's just cut it open." Yelling that she'd be right out, Anna Mae scrambled to get into her clothes. She was still barefoot when she emerged and found herself face to face with FBI agent David Price. "You! You!" he shouted. "I've been looking all over for you. I'm so glad I found you." Directed to stand with the other women, Anna Mae watched the FBI agents ransack the Running home. Belongings crashed to the floor as agents moved larger pieces of furniture, snickering and laughing as they vandalized Running's medicine pouches, eagle feathers, pipes, beadwork and other religious and ceremonial objects.

Meanwhile, David Price questioned Anna Mae and threatened her with deportation, then handcuffed her and took her to jail in Pierre, South Dakota. En route he again told her she was in the country illegally. "You'll be in Canada by this afternoon," he promised. In Pierre, Price and agent Fred Coward had Anna Mae stripped and searched before interrogating her at length. When she was taken from the Running residence that morning, Anna Mae was told she was being charged with the illegal possession of dynamite. In Pierre the charge was changed to possession of a firearm with an obliterated serial number.

When the interrogation began, Anna Mae demanded a lawyer, but her request was refused. She objected and was told, "You're not going to get a call through unless you talk to us first." The agents implied that she did not need a lawyer because the subject of the questioning was not that morning's raid, but the killings of the FBI agents on the Jumping Bull land. Although Anna Mae said she had not been there that day, the agents pressed on, convinced that she knew what had transpired. They insisted that she could tell them where to find Leonard Peltier, Robert Robideau,

Frank Blackhorse and Dennis Banks. Exactly when the FBI decided to charge Butler, Robideau and Peltier with killing the agents is unclear. The Bureau claims it was only after some weeks of investigation, but others say that the three were immediately targeted and with them Anna Mae Aquash.

Butler, who was arrested with Anna Mae on the morning of September 5, had worked with her in organizing AIM's West Coast office and like her was assuming increasing leadership responsibilities within AIM. Peltier had been a fugitive since 1972 when he was accused of attempted murder. He had allegedly pointed a gun he knew would not fire at an off-duty, out-of-uniform police officer, after a dispute in a bar. (He has recently been acquitted of the charge by a jury in Wisconsin.) In Oglala, Peltier had been an effective community organizer. Banks had gone underground in early August 1975, rather than face a South Dakota prison term arising from his conviction on the Custer charges. He cited William Janklow's widely publicized threat against the lives of AIM leaders as one reason he feared for his life in state custody. The state Attorney General who personally prosecuted the case against Banks had said that the only way to deal with AIM leaders was "to put a bullet through their heads". Frank Blackhorse had been sought since his failure to appear for a scheduled court hearing in May 1975.

An FBI summary of the interrogation states that when she was asked if she knew the four men the FBI were seeking, Anna Mae put her head down on the desk and said, "You can either shoot me or throw me in jail, as those are the two choices I am taking." When the agents asked her to explain she added, "That's what you're going to do with me anyway." In court the next morning Anna Mae refused to plead guilty, and although it was her first arrest, bail was set at $5,000. In a personal statement to the court she described the work she had been doing in Oglala since the spring. After a brief discussion, the judge refused to lower her bail, believing she had been indicted by the grand jury which was considering evidence relating to the June 26 shootings. When her court-appointed attorney, Robert Riter, finally spoke up and it became clear she had not been indicted, she was allowed to post ten per cent of the bail. The first arrested, Anna Mae was also the first released, but the outstanding criminal charge made her an easier target for FBI harassment.

Almost immediately she called her sister, Rebecca Julian. In past years Anna Mae had visited her daughters at least once a year, and it had been a year since she had done so. This year was different. "I've been in jail," she told her sister, after warning her to speak in Micmac so they would not be understood on wiretaps. The elder sister reacted with surprise. "What for?" she demanded. Perhaps fearing sharp words, Anna Mae drew back. She spoke of friends who had been charged "with something they didn't do", and told Rebecca she feared for her own life. "Then why don't you come home?" her sister asked. "Why are you staying there?"

Anna Mae had often talked of returning to Nova Scotia, getting legal custody of her daughters and settling down. Bruce Ellison, the WKLDOC attorney, was helping her with the custody case, but the work in Oglala always came first. "If you could see the people, the way they're treated here, you'd understand," she told her sister. Rebecca Julian did not understand. Nor did she understand when Anna Mae said, "These woods are full of men. They're out to get me. They'll kill me if the FBI doesn't get me first." Rebecca Julian was never able to get clarification of this statement.

Anna Mae had often spoken to friends about her premonitions of personal danger. As early as 1973, following her participation in the occupation of Wounded Knee, she told one close friend that she felt she did not have long to live. Those who participated in the occupation often express their suspicions that the FBI has a list of participants who have been targeted by the agency. Anna Mae may have had that in mind when she told her friend, "They'll execute me. That's what they do to Indians who fight for their people." What may have been an exaggeration in 1973 was no longer such in 1975 when she told her attorney Bruce Ellison that she feared for her life. By that time she knew too much—about AIM, its programs, plans and leadership. Other friends say she told them she had been threatened by FBI agent

David Price following the Rosebud raid. He allegedly told her that if she did not cooperate in their investigation of the agents' deaths she would not live out the year. "The FBI agents made her the same offer they made me that day at Pierre, after I too was arrested and transported there from Al Running's home," wrote Darelle Butler from his jail cell. "Cooperate and live, don't cooperate you die."

Anna Mae returned to Rapid City to help with fundraising for those still in jail. On September 13 she flew to Los Angeles. When she and Nilak Butler stepped off the plane Butler was arrested, and Anna Mae was again detained for several hours. That same weekend FBI agents in Kansas had arrested eight AIM supporters, among them 20-year-old Kamook Banks and 29-year-old Robert Robideau. The group had been driving on the turnpike near Wichita, Kansas, when the car exploded. Authorities claimed they were carrying dynamite and grenades. A suspect in the June 26 slayings, Robideau was hospitalized and then held on $125,000 bond. Two months later he was charged with the murder of Coler and Williams. The FBI was closing its net. In Rapid City and Minneapolis there were yet more arrests of AIM supporters.

On the West Coast Anna Mae is said to have joined Dennis Banks, Peltier and others. Her ability to play whatever part the occasion demanded meant she was often the one who would "surface" to make the ncessary arrangements to keep the others beyond the reach of the FBI. At this time she was also working to develop a proposal to raise funds for an AIM national newspaper.

Anna Mae returned to South Dakota in early October for her arraignment on two felony charges brought against her by a grand jury following the Rosebud raid. In Oglala Anna Mae showed her friend Dorothy Brings'Em Back a letter from her court-appointed attorney Robert Riter, offering her a deal: if she would testify against Darelle and Nilak Butler before the grand jury investigating the shootings of FBI agents Coler and Williams, one felony charge would be dropped and she could plead guilty to the other. "I think Riter really thought it was a good deal," AIM attorney Bruce Ellison said later. Anna Mae refused it and gave the letter to Brings 'Em Back. "If you think it's important, keep it," she told her and then left. Anna Mae returned furtively to Oglala one night shortly thereafter saying, "Dennis sent me to get $150 from you. Can you do it?" The Oglala women spent a day trying, but could raise only half the amount. Anna Mae took it and disappeared.

When Anna Mae next called the WKLDOC office at the end of October, she was wrongly told that there were no court appearances scheduled for her. Thus when she failed to appear for an early November hearing of pre-trial motions in Pierre, South Dakota, a bench warrant was issued for her arrest. At that moment she officially became a federal fugitive charged with violations of the firearms law.

Two weeks later, the Portland, Oregon office of the FBI alerted area police agencies to be on the lookout for a Dodge Explorer motor home with New Mexico licence plates travelling with a white station wagon. The motor home, owned by actor Marlon Brando, was said to be transporting fugitives Dennis Banks, Leonard Peltier and others. Oregon state troopers stopped the vehicles on the night of November 14 on Interstate Highway 80 near Ontario, Oregon not far from the Idaho border.

Russell Redner and Kenneth Loudhawk, travelling in the station wagon, submitted to arrest without resistance. Anna Mae Aquash, Kamook Banks, eight months pregnant and carrying her year-old daughter, and a man said to be Leonard Peltier, descended from the motor home on the troopers' orders. Suddenly the motor home sped off down the highway as the unidentified man ran off, turning to fire a shot in the direction of the state troopers before he disappeared and forcing the women and child face down onto the pavement to avoid the gunfire. The two women were arrested but not charged immediately, although both later faced multiple-count state and federal indictments as a result of the incident. Both were detained for transfer to other jurisdictions. According to one report, David Price was among the FBI agents at the police station where Anna Mae and her companions were taken following their arrest on the Oregon interstate.

Anna Mae was held in Vale, Oregon and then in Vancouver, Washington while awaiting extradition to South Dakota. She told an Idaho reporter, "If they take me back to South Dakota, I'll be murdered." To her sister Rebecca Julian she wrote, "South Dakota is a very racist state, I am sure I will be sent up even though it is my first arrest.... I knew that it would come.... My efforts to raise the consciousness of whites that are so against Indians here in the United States were bound to be stopped by the FBI....

"These white people think this country belongs to them—they don't realize they are only in charge right now because there's more of them than there are of us. This whole country changed with only a handful of raggedy-ass pilgrims that came over here in the 1500s. And it can take a handful of raggedy-ass Indians to do the same, and I intend to be one of those raggedy-ass Indians."

Fearing that her daughters might grow up believing she was "no good", she instructed Rebecca to save her letters "so that when my girls are of age they can read [them] and know the real truth....I'm not going to stop fighting for my country until I die—and then my kids will take over....My heart hurts so badly every time I think of my girls."

Anna Mae was taken in chains to Pierre, South Dakota, where on November 24 she appeared before Judge Robert Mehrige, who had earned a reputation as a Liberal in civil rights cases. To her surprise she was not unduly harassed. When he heard the reason for her previous failure to appear on the firearms charges, Judge Mehrige appeared sympathetic and released her into the custody of her lawyer for trial the next day. Prosecuting attorney R.D. Hurd did not indulge in the histrionics AIM members had come to expect from him; usually he argued vehemently that the accused was "a danger to society" and ought to remain in official custody. Anna Mae's treatment in Oregon—the chains, the large complement of officers and the strict security during her transfer—had seemed to confirm that the government regarded her as very dangerous indeed.

That night, Anna Mae received a phone call from a friend and some time later walked out of what should have been a carefully-watched motel room, stepped into a car and headed west. The following day charges against her co-defendants in the September 5 Rosebud incident were dismissed because the government could not prove prior knowledge or ownership of the weapons found in the tent she had shared with several others. Had she not fled, Anna Mae might have been a free woman. Instead, enraged at her failure to appear, Judge Mehrige issued a bench warrant for her arrest.

Almost immediately, however, came word of a ten-count indictment handed down against Anna Mae and others involved in the Oregon incident and a South Dakota grand jury charged her Rosebud co-defendant Darelle Butler with first-degree murder in the June 26 shooting deaths of FBI agents Coler and Williams.

The events of November 24-25 and the narrow escape of men alleged to be Banks and Peltier in Oregon rekindled rumours that Anna Mae Aquash was an FBI spy. The November 14 arrests resulted from information given to police by someone who apparently had been at the Washington State encampment where the motor home's ill-fated journey began. Furthermore, Anna Mae had been the first person released after the Rosebud raid, her detractors argued. Her effortless departure from Pierre the night of November 24 was also difficult to explain. Later the attorney who represented her in court, Robert Riter, said he was told casually by police officials involved in the case that they knew where his missing client went.

Anna Mae, however, had no reason to believe the charges against her would be dismissed on November 25. She knew the FBI wanted information from her. She also knew she would face additional charges as a result of the Oregon incident, further complicating her legal position. When Anna Mae wrote Rebecca Julian five days earlier, she advised her sister to "call Rapid City after Monday, November 24 to find out how I made out". But when her chance came to escape she took it. In doing so she may unwittingly have served the purposes of the FBI. Her friends believe that the Bureau allowed her to flee hoping she would lead them to the fugitives they really wanted—Dennis Banks and Leonard Peltier. As the FBI manhunt intensified, tension and suspicion among AIM members increased. It was clear that there were informers with access to many of the movement's plans and activities. The bulk of suspicion fell on Anna Mae Aquash, and this time the accusations were taken seriously.

In early December, Anna Mae was brought from Denver, Colorado for questioning by AIM in Rapid City, South Dakota.

As one person after another came in to talk to her she began to cry. There was no case against her and when she was released she went to the West Coast. There, despite her fugitive status and the accusations against her, she continued to work for AIM. On December 20, she called her friend Paula Giese in Minneapolis and indicated that she would be in Minneapolis-St. Paul by January. She told Giese, who had helped in the exposure of Durham and had subsequently researched his background, that she had information about events on the West Coast that would interest her. Giese was becoming personally involved in the defence of Paul Skyhorse and Richard Mohawk, the AIM organizers charged with the brutal murder of cabby George Aird. Anna Mae did not reach Minneapolis.

Rumours that she spent the Christmas of 1975 with friends on Pine Ridge have never been confirmed. She also failed to make her traditional Christmas phone calls to her daughters, sisters and close friend in Nova Scotia. So accustomed were they to hearing from her that they began to fear something was seriously wrong.

Meanwhile in Minneapolis-St. Paul, WKLDOC attorneys were still speculating on the possibility that Anna Mae was spying for the FBI. "If she's a pig, she's the best one the government ever had," one lawyer reportedly remarked. Whatever the accusation against her, Anna Mae never acted according to the usual informer pattern. It was more common for a spy to be an unobtrusive person on the periphery of AIM or, if active, a disruptive force. Anna Mae Aquash was neither; the work she did undoubtedly benefitted AIM and the accusations against her were based entirely on speculation.

On January 16, 1976, fugitive Dennis Banks was arrested on an informer's tip at the home of California professor Lehman Brightman. So interested was the FBI in protecting the identity of that informer that it refused to press charges against Brightman—which would have meant revealing the source of their information—even though the case against him for harbouring a fugitive was clear-cut. Later, during preparation for the trials of Banks, his wife Kamook, Russell Redner and Kenneth Loudhawk on charges stemming from the Oregon shoot-out, the FBI released an affidavit showing that there had been not one but two informers prior to the November 14 arrests. It was apparently so important to the FBI that the identities of the pair be kept secret that evidence purportedly obtained at the time of the arrests—a quantity of dynamite—was destroyed by officials prior to the trial, resulting in the dismissal of charges against the four accused. The government was not able to proceed with its case without identifying its informers, it is believed.

Information from informers also led to the arrest of the two remaining AIM fugitives, Frank Blackhorse and Leonard Peltier, at Smallboy's spiritual camp near Hinton, Alberta on February 6, 1976. With those two arrests the FBI had in custody the major AIM leaders, including the three persons—Leonard Peltier, Darelle Butler and Robert Robideau—indicted in the June 26 shootings of agents Coler and Williams.

Speculation within AIM about the role of Anna Mae Aquash intensified further. One theory was that she had been a clandestine partner to Douglass Durham, part of the kind of male-female spy team favoured by the FBI. The circumstantial evidence was superficially convincing: Anna Mae had been at all the AIM actions and close to the AIM leaders then in jail. The FBI had sought her for information about the June 26 killings. Perhaps, it was argued, they had persuaded her to provide that information. Anna Mae was the key to the arrests, the mystery informer.

Rumours about spies and informers were given still further impetus by the return of Douglass Durham. In the winter months of 1975-76, Durham was travelling through South Dakota and neighbouring states on a lecture tour sponsored by the John Birch Society. Durham argued, as he would later do before the Eastland committee, that AIM was a dangerous and subversive organization, infiltrated by communists.

On Pine Ridge Reservation, meanwhile, tribal chairman Richard Wilson was defeated in elections held early in January 1976 but would not leave office until early spring. On January 31, Wilson supporters invaded the settlement of Wanblee and staged a weekend of violence during which AIM supporter Byron De Sersa was murdered. The goons were apparently making good earlier threats to "straighten out" those who did not support Wilson in the elections. Residents of Wanblee, like those of other outlying districts had, despite the threats, voted overwhelmingly for Wilson's successor, Al Trimble.

By mid-February 1976 the FBI had captured all the outstanding AIM fugitives and was intent on building its case against those indicted in the June 26 slayings. On January 31, 1976, under threats from FBI agents that he would "never walk the earth again", 16-year-old Norman Brown, an AIM member, lied to the grand jury investigating the murders. On February 19, Myrtle Poor Bear, an Indian woman from Allen, South Dakota was interrogated by FBI agents David Price and William Wood and signed a completely false affidavit in which she claimed to have been present on the Jumping Bull land the day the agents were shot. On February 23, and again on March 31, Poor Bear signed another bogus affidavit, claiming this time to have witnessed the shootings. The following day, February 24, 1976, she was to have been interrogated by agents Price and Wood, but was instead questioned by agent Fred Skelly because Price and Wood were called away to another case. The affidavits Poor Bear signed would later be used to secure the extradition from Canada of Leonard Peltier.

During the week of February 24, 1976, Poor Bear's family, unaware of her whereabouts for some time, heard that an unidentified Indian woman had been found dead near Wanblee. Family members travelled to Pine Ridge Hospital to determine if the as yet unidentified woman was their daughter and sister. Unknown to them, Myrtle Poor Bear was at that time being held incommunicado by the FBI. More than a year passed before Poor Bear revealed that she had been shown pictures of the dead woman, Anna Mae Aquash, and told that if she did not cooperate, the same thing would happen to her.

9/The Persecution and Execution of Anna Mae Aquash

Sioux elders say the winds always howl when the body of a murder victim is moved. During the traditional wake and funeral given Anna Mae Aquash the week-end of March 12, 1976, a storm peaked, sending 30-mile-per-hour winds blasting across the desolate fields and shaking the rickety Jumping Bull Hall where the wake was being held. The unseasonal thaw that three weeks before had led to the discovery of Anna Mae's body had given way to a bitter cold. The corpse awaited its second burial bound in blankets and robes, resting on a log pole bier inside a canvas-covered teepee near the rickety building known as Jumping Bull Hall. Indian youths took axes to the government-supplied coffin and burned it in a bonfire outside. Periodically a police helicopter and a police airplane flew low over the wake site but there were no incidents.

The weather worsened and the mourners huddled around two wood stoves improvised from 50-gallon drums, which provided slight comfort against the winds tearing through the cardboard sheathing of the hall. When it seemed the entire building might collapse, the funeral bier was moved into the one-room cabin where Dennis Banks had lived the previous summer, and the mourners moved into the abandoned Jumping Bull residence, site of the bloody FBI-Indian shoot-out eight months before. Many of those present were elderly Sioux women, dark shawls framing their lined faces: they had witnessed many funerals in the last few years.

Above the funeral bier hung the AIM flag and a photocopy of a newspaper picture showing Anna Mae Aquash chained waist-to-waist with Kamook Banks after their arrest in Oregon. Sacred flags of yellow, black, white and red, representing the four winds, hung around the bier. On top of it were the presents of cigarettes, tobacco, beaded clothes and moccasins that Anna Mae would take to the other world.

It was snowing heavily by the time Anna Mae's sisters, Mary Lafford and Rebecca Julian, arrived in Oglala on Sunday, March 13. They watched in stunned silence as additional prayers were offered by the Sioux medicine men. To the sound of the drum, the chants and the sobbing wails, six young Indian men wearing red headbands stepped forward, lifted the bier and carried it to the rear of an open station wagon outside. The funeral cortege of 75 cars and pick-up trucks followed the station wagon to the grave site on Wallace Little's ranch a few miles east on Highway 18. The graves on the hill-top plot already told of the tragedies of life and death on Pine Ridge. Two years before, the first grave had been dug for Little's son, killed by a white man in Florida. In June 1975, the second grave was dug for Joe Stuntz, killed in the shoot-out on the Jumping Bull land. A few months later another of Little's sons was buried there, after being kicked to death in Oglala in a fight over a pair of spurs. The fourth grave, for Anna Mae Aquash, had been excavated the night before by four young Oglala women, one of whom lay down in the hole to measure it. "We might as well learn to bury each other," Roslyn Jumping Bull had told the other women, "because nobody else will help us."

The sacred colours were tied to stakes at each corner of the grave. The wind whipped the upside-down American flag that hung next to the two medicine men praying to the four winds in the Sioux way. The mourners threw down presents to be entombed with the dead woman. Gesturing with the sacred pipe and bundles of sage, the medicine men directed the pall bearers to pick up their shovels.

Back at the Jumping Bull house the colourful knitted AIM flag was given to Mary Lafford to take back to Mary Ellen Barlow in

New Brunswick. Anna Mae's two young daughters had been kept home in Halifax by their father, Jake Maloney. Nogeeshik Aquash was not at the funeral, nor were any of the AIM leaders Anna Mae had been close to during her life. Darelle Butler was in a South Dakota jail, charged with the murders of the two FBI agents. Leonard Peltier was in a Canadian jail, fighting extradition to South Dakota on the same charge. Vernon Bellecourt phoned Rapid City several times from Minneapolis saying he would attend the funeral, but did not. Russell Means, his brother and friends were attending a basketball game a few miles away but they came to neither the wake nor the funeral. Dennis Banks was still in California fighting extradition to South Dakota where a jail term awaited him for his participation in the Custer confrontation of 1973. Although he had called Mary Lafford to offer his condolences it was several days before he declared the day of Anna Mae's funeral a national Indian day of mourning.

The sluggish response to Anna Mae's funeral revealed the extent to which the rumour campaign linking Anna Mae to the FBI had been effective. The widespread suspicion about her accounts in large part for the delayed reaction from AIM leaders and the WKLDOC support group and for the difficulties faced by Anna Mae's personal friends when they sought the exhumation of her body and the second autopsy, which revealed she had been murdered. The paralyzed response of AIM to the Aquash tragedy was in part due to the belief that she might have been killed by a member of the organization. Dennis Banks reportedly initiated an investigation and then called it off because, in his words, "If AIM was involved, it would crush our movement." This reluctance to seek the truth carried its own price, however.

Among some AIM members, particularly the women who had been Anna Mae's friends, the death created a desire to get as far away from AIM as possible. Some felt it was dangerous to defend the dead woman, fearing that anyone who did so would be labelled an informer. Thus the already battered movement suffered another severe blow. According to Paula Giese, "Anna Mae's death did not destroy AIM. What it did was show that AIM was dead." While this harsh opinion is not shared by all AIM members or supporters, the Aquash death marked a very low point in the organization's affairs.

The suspicion remains that Anna Mae Aquash was killed by an AIM member, who was convinced she was an informer and murdered her in a desperate attempt to stem the flow of information to the FBI and protect the hunted leaders. There was no precedent for such treatment of informers in the organization, but according to one observer, "If ever there was to be a first, the time was ripe for it."

Friends of the dead woman say she was perfectly capable of defending herself physically and are convinced she would never knowingly entangle herself in a dangerous situation. They point out that Anna Mae Aquash never went anywhere alone. In Oglala she would not walk the mile or so to the nearest store in broad daylight without company. How then did she find herself trapped in the situation that led to her murder? The obvious answer seemed to be that Anna Mae had been uncharacteristically careless or that at the time she was apprehended by the murderer, or murderers, she was in the company of someone she knew and trusted.

In time, however, AIM leaders began to overcome their previous doubts about Anna Mae as new information came to light and as they observed the FBI's actions in the case. Later in 1976 Dennis Banks sent his representatives to the Pine Ridge Reservation. They brought back information which led Banks to conclude that it wasn't "our people" who killed her. Indian people were further encouraged by the spiritual ceremonies conducted after Aquash's death which produced a claim that she was killed by three persons—two white men and a reluctant Indian.

It remains for the murder investigation to uncover the actual circumstances of the murder, but, the FBI's investigation has failed to provide the answer. In fact, the FBI seems to have done what it can to propagate the view that Anna Mae Aquash was the victim of AIM retaliation. The FBI initially publicized the information that AIM was suspicious of the dead woman. The reference came in the March 8 affidavit of agent William Wood, with which the Bureau sought permission to exhume the body. The source of the FBI information, Anna Mae Tanequodle, a Tulsa, Oklahoma woman known to AIM as Ella Mae Tanegule, was herself widely suspected of supplying information to the FBI to avoid prosecution on prostitution charges. Then, on March 11, *before* the results of the second autopsy were known, a story appeared in the *Rapid City Journal*, captioned "FBI Denies AIM Implication That Aquash Was Informant". In this way the Bureau, responding publicly to charges that AIM had not made public, set the stage for its interpretation of a murder that had not yet been officially discovered.

Further questions were raised by the FBI's subsequent investigation. Indian people who knew Anna Mae Aquash on Pine Ridge Reservation say they have not been questioned about her death. Dr. Steven Shanker and nurse Inez Hodges, both of whom examined the body before the first autopsy, were not questioned by the FBI until after their names appeared in a *Minneapolis Tribune* story in May 1976. Hodges said they were surprised at the long delay and kept expecting the police to question them. The FBI says it didn't know the pair had relevant information so didn't question them till after the *Tribune* article was published. The one AIM supporter who was called to give testimony before a grand jury investigating the Aquash murder was Selo Black Crow, a spiritual leader from Wanblee. He had never met the dead woman; but, in the eight months between the June 26 shootings and the discovery of Anna Mae's body, he had been harassed by the FBI on a number of occasions. All other witnesses before the grand jury, which heard evidence in March 1976, were apparently goons and FBI agents. This caused AIM observers to conclude that the investigation was designed to come to a predetermined conclusion, implicating one of its members. Selo Black Crow thought the FBI was trying to pin it on him. Some friends and acquaintances of Anna Mae Aquash who did not live on Pine Ridge were contacted by the FBI. One family was offered $4,000 for information about Aquash after agents gained entry to their home by pretending to be encyclopedia salesmen. Another individual was shown a wad of $1,000 bills with the implication that they would be his in return for the right kind of information.

FBI statements forwarded to the Canadian government clearly indicate that the American authorities thought the answers to the murder lay within AIM. In a statement filed in the House of Commons in December 1976, the FBI attributed its failure to come up with leads in the case to non-cooperation from AIM members and other Pine Ridge Reservation residents. It cited the instance of an acquaintance of the dead woman who was "purposely eluding" contact with the FBI. If this is in fact the reason for the Bureau's inability to solve the murder, it has only itself to blame. The FBI's entire modus operandi on the reservation since Wounded Knee, and particularly after the June 26 shoot-out; its non-investigation of the January 31 murder of AIM supporter Byron De Sersa, who was killed by reservation goons; and its treatment of witnesses in the Coler-Williams case provide obvious reasons for an uncooperative attitude from AIM members and reservation residents. The history of FBI-AIM relations suggests that if the Bureau really thought the culprit were an AIM member it would have done everything in its power to apprehend that person, leaving no stone unturned.

The possibility of the FBI conducting an impartial investigation into the case of Anna Mae Aquash is also brought into question by FBI actions that predate the murder by almost a year. What, for example, was the FBI's interest in Anna Mae that led agents to subject her to what was apparently an harassing interrogation well before the June 26 shoot-out? What interest led the FBI to search out former associates and to trace one individual through the RCMP to a remote town in the Maritimes?

Some within AIM believe that it was John Stewart who first began spreading rumours that Anna Mae was an informer, some time before the June 26 killings. Stewart, alias Darryl Blue Lake, had helped man the roadblocks set up around Wounded Knee by tribal chairman Richard Wilson and his goons in 1973. Sometime before June 26, 1975 he forced his way back into the Oglala home of his ex-wife. Although he had no job and no apparent income, Stewart volunteered his car to WKLDOC workers on the reservation and soon became a willing AIM chauffeur. Following the September 5 raid in Rosebud he helped transport some AIM members to Denver. He later left South Dakota for a tour of the north-western states and Canada, allegedly in his own car. Suspicions about him were already aroused when AIM chapters in these areas phoned Pine Ridge asking about Stewart and reporting his sometimes disruptive behaviour. Stewart came back to the reservation on or about November 25, 1975. He appeared on the list of prosecution witnesses during the 1976 trial of Robert Robideau and Darelle Butler, charged with shooting the two agents. He did not testify but was escorted back to the reservation by FBI agents. Soon the word was out in Pine Ridge that John Stewart was an FBI informer, a belief that remains despite Stewart's public denial of the charge. He has since disappeared from the area.

Questions about what seems to have been an unusual FBI interest in Anna Mae Aquash in the spring of 1975 were heightened when Stewart's role in undermining her reputation was noted. Some AIM members subsequently came to believe that Aquash had become a target for FBI harassment well before the June 26 shoot-out. Although there is no conclusive proof, they believe that her rising stature within AIM as well as her close relationship with AIM leaders may have made her a target. Following the June 26 killings, the FBI hunted Anna Mae Aquash for two months, apparently believing she knew who had killed agents Coler and Williams and extending the search into Canada. When the FBI finally caught up with her on September 5, she was arrested on a flimsy charge, then questioned about the events of June 26 and the whereabouts of AIM leaders the FBI was seeking. Aquash refused to cooperate in the investigation. As a result, according to this theory, the FBI intensiified the efforts to undermine her credibility within AIM, making sure she was the first released following the September 5 raid. Through her attorney Robert Riter she was offered a deal, another chance to cooperate. Again she refused. On November 24, after being brought to Pierre, South Dakota in chains and under heavy guard, she was allowed to flee her motel room. This, according to proponents of the snitch-jacket theory, was designed to make it look as if she were getting special favours. At the same time the FBI apparently kept tabs on her whereabouts, perhaps hoping she would lead them to the fugitives,

Banks and Peltier. If in fact the FBI created a snitch-jacket for Anna Mae Aquash, it was a successful ploy; by December, suspicion about her had reached an all time high.

What happened next is unclear. Aquash is rumoured to have been on the Pine Ridge Reservation at Christmas, but these rumours are denied in Pine Ridge. Her family in Nova Scotia believes she may already have been in some kind of difficulty or else she would certainly have contacted them during the holidays. Aquash's whereabouts in late December 1975 and in January and February 1976 continue to be a mystery. It was during this time that the FBI intensified its search for, and finally arrested, Banks and Peltier. Suspicion about Aquash increased still more. It was also during this time that the FBI was building its case against Peltier, Butler and Robideau, forcing witnesses to testify and perjure themselves.

What happened to Anna Mae Aquash during this time? Some suggest that she was again picked up by the FBI and again refused to cooperate, a refusal that led to her death. "I believe the FBI carried out their promise [to kill her if she didn't cooperate] to her," wrote Darelle Butler from jail. AIM's most compelling argument in making these charges was and still is the behaviour of the FBI and the BIA police following the discovery of Anna Mae's body near Wanblee. None of the questions about official action in the period from February 24 to March 11, 1976 has ever been answered. Attempts by AIM attorney Ken Tilsen and the U.S. Commission on Civil Rights to obtain clarification of those procedures have been met with Justice Department and FBI stonewalling. This official reticence has been justified on the ground that a murder investigation is still underway.

Anna Mae Aquash knew that her life was in danger because she knew too much about AIM and its operations. To one friend she remarked obscurely, "I can't tell everything I know to one person. But if someone follows carefully in my footsteps they will learn what I know." What had she learned that she wanted to relay to friends in Minneapolis-St. Paul? Had she finally discovered something relating to AIM's West Coast operations and its problems there?

Evidence that the FBI has been conducting a campaign of disruption against AIM and its members cannot be ignored. An investigation by the Senate Committee on Intelligence which might have documented this campaign fully was nipped in the bud by the shootings of June 26, 1975. There has been no attempt to resume it. It might be that such an investigation, undertaken now, would reveal important information relating to the murder of Anna Mae Aquash. It might be that a search of the FBI's file on the dead woman—apparently code-named the Brave Hearted Woman—if done by an independent, external investigator would answer questions about FBI activities in relation to Anna Mae. Civil litigation remains a possibility, though this approach received a setback when a United States federal court judge recently dismissed the suit brought against police officials by the families of Black Panther leaders Fred Hampton and Mark Clark. The suit had brought out many details of questionable police behaviour in relation to the shooting deaths of the two men.

Anna Mae's sister Mary Lafford, meanwhile, believes that justice will not be served and that her sister's murderer will never be found or punished. On Pine Ridge Reservation, however, a thread of optimism remains. "Indian people know everything happens twice," said an old Lakota woman when asked about the Aquash murder. "It always takes five years for the truth to come out, but it always comes out."

10/Quiet Canadians, Quiet Diplomacy

The murder of Anna Mae Aquash and the circumstances leading to it involve an extremely complex series of events, but in a sense the case is simple. Anna Mae Aquash was a "radical" Indian who participated in the infamous Wounded Knee occupation. She was a national leader in the American Indian Movement. She was also a Canadian citizen with relatives in Nova Scotia, New Brunswick and Ontario, who was murdered in a foreign country. After an incomplete autopsy, her body was mutilated and illegally buried.

Had some other Canadian citizen suffered a similar fate there would have been a significant reaction from the Canadian media, the public and the government. In the case of Anna Mae Aquash there was almost none. In South Dakota superficial news stories, based primarily on FBI reports, followed the second autopsy. A more complete story was carried in Indian newspapers in Canada and the United States.

The murder of Anna Mae Aquash and that of Byron De Sersa on January 31, 1976 were investigated by the United States Commission on Civil Rights. In a lengthy memo from chairman Arthur Fleming to the Justice Department, the commission demanded explanations of the unusual circumstances surrounding both deaths and the widespread violations of civil rights on Pine Ridge Reservation.

> Because of the manner in which FBI agents allegedly handled the recent murders of Anna Mae Aquash and Byron De Sersa, along with the record of an extraordinary number of

unresolved homicides and incidents of terror and violence which have become unfortunately commonplace, the sentiment prevails that life is cheap on the Pine Ridge Reservation....Reports of improprieties by the FBI which reached us are of a serious nature and if found to be true should be corrected immediately....We again...request that you assess the activities of the FBI on the Pine Ridge Reservation....

The Commission received a perfunctory response. "We have reviewed the FBI's investigation of the death of Anna Mae Aquash," a Department of Justice spokesman wrote. "Although the first autopsy is subject to criticism, we have found no evidence of any attempt to conceal the cause of death, nor any evidence of misconduct by the FBI." AIM attorney Kenneth Tilsen outlined in detail his concerns about police performance from the time the body of Anna Mae Aquash was found until the completion of the second autopsy in a letter sent to FBI Director Clarence Kelley and Attorney General Edward Levi. It too was virtually ignored.

The American Indian Movement, to which Anna Mae Aquash had dedicated her life, was slow to react for reasons already noted. Canadian External Affairs officials, who might have been expected to issue some statement, however routine, concerning the murder of a Canadian citizen, said nothing. Had it not been for the Toronto meeting of the Canadian Friends' Service Committee and its Committee on Native Concerns (QCNC), the Canadian public might never have heard about the case of Anna Mae Aquash. On February 6, 1976 the Quakers were asked by AIM spiritual leader Art Solomon of Sudbury for their help in finding lawyers for Leonard Peltier and Frank Blackhorse, who had that day been arrested near Hinton, Alberta. In the weeks following, while trying to gather information about Peltier and the crime with which he was charged—the murder of FBI agents Coler and Williams—the QCNC first heard the shocking story of Anna Mae Aquash.

On March 23, the New Brunswick Union of Indians, acting for Anna Mae's mother, had asked the Department of External Affairs to investigate the Aquash murder, with no apparent result.

On April 21, the QCNC and four other organizations wrote to Allan MacEachen, then Minister of External Affairs, urging an immediate inquiry into the case to find specific answers to the many questions surrounding the murder. MacEachen, coincidentally, is Member of Parliament for the riding in which the dead woman's sisters and daughters lived.

No Canadian daily newspaper reported on the five organizations' press conference April 21 or on a public meeting April 24 at which AIM lawyer Kenneth Tilsen, who was by then representing the family, outlined details of the case. An interview with Minneapolis reporter Kevin McKiernan on April 27 prompted the CBC's Peter Gzowski to comment that MPs should be asking questions about the case in the House of Commons. Two days later Conservative MP Gordon Fairweather did just that, but received no reply for a month. Publicity increased during May, reaching a high point with the *Washington Star*'s headline story detailing the curious events surrounding the death of the Wounded Knee veteran. A *Minneapolis Tribune* story a few days later raised still further, more disturbing questions about the case.

The Canadian media, however, continued to display little interest in the story, leading Barry Zwicker of *Content* magazine to make a cutting analysis of the racial attitudes of his Canadian journalistic colleagues: "[The Aquash] murder case, one suspects, would have been more readily identified as news had the victim been a middle-class white...." Zwicker illustrated his point with references to the extensive press coverage of a Canadian businessman unjustly detained in Mexico at about the same time.

Canadian officials, meanwhile, promised much but did little. Responding to a House of Commons question from MP Wally Firth on May 14, External Affairs Minister Allan MacEachen said: "I have instructed our embassy in Washington to ask the United States for an urgent investigation into the circumstances of this case, which...raises many questions of very great concern." When MacEachen was asked on June 29 if he had received any report from United States officials, he replied in the affirmative, but the report he made public was a copy of an FBI press release issued by Director Clarence Kelley on May 26. MacEachen was also asked about the status of the U.S. Justice Department investigation into the FBI handling of the case. He promised to follow up that part of the question but it was never answered, perhaps because there was no serious Justice Department investigation. Letters received by the U.S. Civil Rights Commission indicate the Justice Department asked the FBI and the U.S. Attorney in South Dakota as well as its own civil rights division if there were any truth to the allegations of misconduct. The reply, not surprisingly, was negative.

Five months later, Wally Firth asked newly-appointed External Affairs Minister Donald Jamieson for an update. He received no immediate reply, but a month later Jamieson tabled another two-page FBI report. The report, which the Canadian government received on December 15, 1976, contained almost word-for-word the May 26 FBI press release. Two additional paragraphs stated that 16 FBI offices, 175 agents and the FBI laboratory and its personnel had been used to investigate the death of Anna Mae Aquash. More than 200 persons were contacted or interviewed, it said, but lack of cooperation from those who knew the victim hampered the FBI's search. "An associate of the victim who allegedly has information regarding the victim's murder...had purposely eluded any contact with the FBI," the report concluded. The Canadian government accepted these meagre reports as a sufficient gesture and continued to accept as fact information from the very U.S. agency whose actions were being questioned and criticized. It was as if the Canadian government were completely unaware of the work of the Church committee of the U.S. Senate and its revelations of extensive FBI misconduct.

Persistent questioning of External Affairs and Justice Department officials by the QCNC in fall 1976 continued to elicit the same kinds of response with slight variations. In one such reply, the QCNC was told that little more information could be provided because a South Dakota grand jury "continues to have this matter under active investigation". When the QCNC sought more information about the grand jury it was given misleading and erroneous information by both the Justice and External Affairs departments. The Canadian officials said that the South Dakota grand jury was set up after the death of Anna Mae Aquash and formed in part as a result of Canadian pressure on the United States. This grand jury did not have the power to indict, they said, but its findings would be made available to Canada. The officials, who at the time were concerned primarily with the Peltier extradition case, apparently did not know that the grand jury investigating the Aquash case in fact had been set up in the spring of 1975. It apparently heard testimony about the Aquash murder for only two or three days in April 1976. It was disbanded at the end of its 18-month term and no reports of its findings were supplied to Canadian authorities.

In the spring of 1977, External Affairs officers continued to insist that "regular representations" were being made to American authorities but without much hope of success because leads in the case had by then grown cold. "Strong efforts were made to get the Canadian government to press for a swift enquiry at top government levels, [but] no one has been surprised to see what has happened," concluded the newsletter *Quaker Concern.* "The Canadian government continued to respond by relaying the official FBI press releases to the Canadian public."

Ottawa's handling of the Anna Mae Aquash case left the impression that protocol and sovereignty issues hampered Canadian efforts to acquire information. There is, however, a great deal of evidence to indicate that the channels of communication between Canadian and U.S. police agencies and government ministries are not nearly as difficult to navigate as official statements suggest. There appears to be a great deal of information-sharing in connection with the handling of "native militants".

Before the occupation of Wounded Knee, RCMP intelligence forces apparently knew little about the American Indian Movement. W.H. Brant, a former native policing advisor with the Ontario Provincial Police and later assistant to Kenora Crown Attorney Ted Burton, claims the FBI sent the RCMP a telex during the final days of the occupation of Wounded Knee advising the Mounties to investigate border crossings by AIM members. "It caught the RCMP with their pants down," Brant said. "They hadn't even heard of the organization." The RCMP responded quickly, however. On May 16, 1973, just eight days after the last holdout emerged from the occupied South Dakota village, Flora MacDonald, then Conservative Party critic for Indian Affairs, noted in the House of Commons that security officers were questioning members of native organizations across Canada asking them to identify and provide information about native people pictured in photographs which seemed to have been taken at the occupation.

During the next two years surveillance of native groups increased, as did cooperation between American and Canadian police assigned to monitor Indian civil rights groups. Between 1973 and 1975, FBI operative Douglass Durham entered Canada with the permission of the RCMP on at least four occasions and collected information on Canadian native leaders under his cover as an AIM director. The RCMP in the Northwest Territories also knew in 1973 that Dennis Banks and his supporters were hiding out in the community of Rae Lakes, 150 miles from Yellowknife, and helped to force them out by cutting off all deliveries of mail and food to the community, setting the stage for the Durham rescue mission. FBI agents themselves have apparently operated in Canada on a number of occasions. In one such incident during the fall of 1973, two agents questioned an Ottawa Indian woman about individuals who had participated in the Wounded Knee occupation. The woman concluded the pair were FBI agents when they showed her identification cards which said they were based in a Texas office of the Bureau.

Canadian police officials also stepped up their own efforts in relation to native groups. Courses on "native extremism" became part of the training of RCMP officers in the Northwest Territories and the Yukon and mock military exercises were carried out in that region and in northern Manitoba to prepare for combatting "guerrillas". The activities of native groups became the topic for information-sharing and discussion at a Canadian-American police seminar and workshop held in Winnipeg in 1975. Some native leaders believe that the riot squads now set up in many cities have special sections whose function it is to deal specifically with native organizations. Although they lack documented proof, many native leaders in Canada are convinced that their organizations are subject to RCMP spying, and in some cases, harassment and disruption. AIM leaders in Alberta, for example, are aware of covert attempts by the RCMP security service to obtain information about individual leaders. False and irresponsible reports have been issued about the activities of AIM leaders, as when Roy Little Chief went to one band office to check its account books. Word went out he was taking over the office by force and all area police detachments were alerted to stand by. Reporters called the band office to ask about the alleged takeover.

A more serious incident occurred near Cornwall, Ontario on the St. Regis Reserve, which straddles the borders of Ontario, Quebec and New York State. When parents and friends of young Alvin Jock went to the community police station in January 1976 to determine why he had been arrested, 80 riot-equipped Quebec police officers descended on them. Radio stations in neighbouring communities broadcast reports about the successful quelling of an "insurrection" on the reserve. The handful of adults meanwhile had not gained entry to the police station and were outside listening to police officers interrogate the boy, who reported that they "slapped me around".

In early 1976 the Indian Brotherhood of the Northwest Territories was the apparent target for what seems to have been an attempt to disrupt the organization during a leadership struggle. D.H. Mumby, an inspector with the RCMP Security Service in Ottawa, was the source of a rumour that three key native leaders were receiving as much as $100,000 each in return for their silence on the MacKenzie Valley Pipeline issue.

One Sunday morning in early February 1976, Mumby approached his minister, Kent Doe, for an informal chat following a sermon that had touched on the issue of native land claims. Doe had recently returned from the Northwest Territories to become pastor of the parish of Blackburn Hamlet, the east Ottawa suburb that is home to a large number of RCMP staff. He was involved in organizing an informational workshop on land claims and maintained regular contact with the NWT Indian Brotherhood. Mumby himself had recently returned from a tour of duty in Latin America in connection with security arrangements for the 1976 Olympics. After telling the minister that "if I lived in South America I'd be a guerrilla", Mumby informed Doe of the three supposedly corrupt native leaders. He asked that Doe not use his name if he relayed the information to his contacts among native people. Doe said NWT Brotherhood members seemed surprised when he told them of the information some time later.

When Brotherhood members learned that Mumby was the source of the information, they sought further details which the RCMP officer refused to provide. Further investigations by the Brotherhood and by reporters to whom they passed on the rumour failed to uncover any substantiating information. Brotherhood members say they decided to ignore the rumour and concentrate on building their support base. Kent Doe continues to believe the information was legitimate. He believes that as a security officer, Mumby would be capable of using such disruptive tactics but maintains that "he would never use me, his spiritual leader," for such purposes.

The Security Service has also attempted to recruit strategically placed individuals to act as spies on perfectly legitimate organizations. In one such instance, Ronald Pankiw, Robert Gordon and Lindsay Welch, members of the Security Service then working in Toronto, attempted to recruit a clergyman who frequently travels across Canada and maintains contact with a wide variety of native organizations. The three, working in pairs, visited the clergyman in September 1975 and on February 3, 1976 offering him an unlimited expense account for liquor and free travel anywhere in return for information on meetings he attended. When the minister complained to Mumby, he received no more such visits.

Surveillance of "subversive" organizations and individuals is the mandate of the security service. The native organizations have as their objectives overcoming the second-class status of their people; improving their economic position, their health and social well-being; and encouraging them in the exercise of their civil rights. Apparently such legitimate political activity does not preclude RCMP spying, and apparently the RCMP, like the FBI, does not always draw the fine line between surveillance and disruptive action. Recent disclosures indicate that the RCMP has been keeping the Alberta Indian Association under surveillance, and the Ontario Provincial Police have acknowledged surveillance of the American Indian Movement in that province.

This information, confirming the suspicions of native leaders, emerged in the fall of 1977 as Quebec's Keable inquiry and the federally-appointed McDonald Commission undertook their investigations into alleged RCMP wrong-doing. After RCMP participation in four allegedly illegal acts came to light, then Solicitor General Francis Fox stated that the force had been breaking into private premises for as long as 20 years. It had also been illegally intercepting and opening mail.

These reports were followed closely by allegations that the security service had obtained confidential medical information and distributed it in the hope of disrupting organizations it considered subversive. These included leftists, black and Indian groups. In Alberta the Laycraft Commission discovered that officers in the Department of National Revenue routinely made available to the RCMP supposedly confidential tax information of persons only suspected of being involved in illegal actions.

The Alberta Indian Association, the public discovered, was one of 14 organizations named in a list of subversive groups kept by the RCMP since 1969. Other legal and democratically-organized groups named included the Canadian Union of Public Employees and the National Farmer's Union. Ontario's Provincial Police meanwhile had been conducting surveillance of the Ojibway Warrior Society and other American Indian Movement groups in that province.

It became clear in August 1975 that Indian groups had been targeted by the security service of the RCMP. At that time a secret document prepared for then Solicitor General Warren Allmand was leaked to the press. "The Red Power movement has become the principal threat to Canadian stability," the RCMP document stated, and in a series of unconvincing generalities it went on to link Canadian Indian organizations to American fugitives and international terrorist conspiracies. "The Red Power Movement" did not intend to overthrow the Canadian government, the report admitted; it was working to obtain equal treatment for native people, satisfaction of their land claims and recognition of the social and economic rights of Canadian Indians. The threat to Canadian stability resulted, the report claimed, from the *possibility* of violence that might occur if the demands of Indian groups were not met. There had already been demonstrations, occupations of buildings and roadblocks, it noted; and after 1973, the influence of AIM had allegedly resulted in several violent incidents in Canada.

The more sensational contents of the RCMP report were printed and broadcast with little or no qualification by an uncritical media. The report was "leaked" in the midst of a heated public controversy about the terrorist activities of the Palestine Liberation Organization and the right of its representatives to enter Canada. The contents of the report and the timing of the leak effectively linked the mild political activities of Canadian native organizations with the armed struggle of the PLO, a link which could have no other effect than to reduce public sympathy for native people's struggles. Various native leaders have concluded that the so-called "leak" was in fact a deliberate release of misinformation.

Another smear occurred a year later when, in September 1976, the U.S. Senate Subcommittee on Internal Security, headed by Mississippi Senator James Eastland released its report on the American Indian Movement. As previously noted, it was based solely on the testimony of Douglass Durham, who claimed that guns stolen from United States armories were being smuggled into Canada, that secret meetings between AIM and Chinese communists were taking place in Canada and that the organization had buried guns in Kenora's Anicinabe Park. Durham's allegations were refuted but not before both AIM and Canadian native organizations had once again been associated in the mass media with violence and terrorism. The timing of the release of the report was another low blow. Durham testified before the Eastland committee on April 6, 1976, but his testimony was not released until six months later, just before the September 26 appeal hearing scheduled in the extradition case of Leonard Peltier.

In both these cases, the respective police forces were able to disseminate widely damaging misinformation without being obliged to accept direct responsibility for it. The RCMP scare paper on Red Power and later events suggests that first Canadian police officials and then Canadian political and judicial authorities quickly adopted the FBI "line" on AIM. They, therefore, became *de facto* associates in the FBI campaign against the organization. The Canadians' failure to act on the Aquash murder case revealed an excessively trusting attitude toward policy and information emanating from the FBI.

The handling of the Leonard Peltier extradition proceedings throughout 1976 provided a further demonstration of the remarkable absence of independent thinking by the Canadians involved. Peltier sought political asylum in Canada on the grounds that charges against him—the shooting of FBI agents Coler and Williams—were political, stemming from his position as a leader in the American Indian Movement and the FBI's targeting of that organization. His claim was not taken seriously, and Canadian authorities treated him as an extremely dangerous criminal. While awaiting extradition, Peltier was held in solitary confinement in British Columbia's Oakalla prison, his legs shackled even when he was in his cell. The light was kept on 24 hours a day, and he was allowed less than 30 minutes exercise daily.

The serious nature of the charges against Peltier reinforced the impression the FBI had conveyed to Canadian authorities. They included an attempted murder charge dating from 1972 and charges stemming from the Oregon shoot-out in November 1975. It was the charges relating to the shootings of agents Coler and Williams, however, which were the major issue and which reinforced in the minds of the Canadians his image as a dangerous killer. So pervasive was this image that several Indian organizations and otherwise sympathetic Members of Parliament would not consider Peltier's claim that the charges against him were political and refused to support his case.

Peltier was ordered extradited and his appeal was subsequently denied by the federal appeals court. When Justice Minister Ron Basford finally ordered the extradition on December 17, 1976, he too chose to overlook blatantly contradictory evidence in affidavits provided by the U.S. authorities to support their extradition request. Basford argued that since co-defendants Butler and Robideau had been acquitted, Peltier could also expect a fair trial. But to Peltier and his supporters, the previous acquittals meant something else entirely; his trial would be the FBI's last chance to secure a conviction in the slayings of Coler and Williams and the Bureau would redouble its efforts to get that conviction. Peltier was convicted and sentenced to life imprisonment in May 1977. At this writing, the conviction is being appealed in part on the basis of considerable evidence of FBI misconduct in the case.

In Peltier's later trial in the United States, the affidavits signed by Myrtle Poor Bear, a woman from the Pine Ridge Reservation, which were used as major evidence in the extradition hearing, were shown conclusively to be contradictory—and false. They were, in fact, fabricated by the FBI. The failure of Canadian officials to acknowledge the obvious inconsistencies in the information provided by the FBI at the Peltier hearing parallels their failure to press for an adequate explanation of FBI conduct in the case of Anna Mae Aquash. In both instances Canadian authorities regarded information provided by the FBI as inviolate and unquestionable, even when that information was clearly deficient.

In the case of Anna Mae Aquash, the Department of External Affairs, which could have played an important role in defending the dead woman's rights, did not do so. There is no evidence that Canada has expressed any dissatisfaction with the way American authorities have dealt with the murder itself or with the Canadian request for an investigation into FBI handling of the case. Instead, FBI press releases were forwarded to the House of Commons as if they constituted an adequate explanation of the case. The failure to think and act independently characterized the Canadian performance every step of the way and dovetailed perfectly with the FBI's strategy to discredit AIM. The desire for continued harmonious relations with American law enforcement agencies apparently overrode the right of Anna Mae's family and the Canadian public to a reasonable pursuit of justice in the case.

Ironically, many Canadians who would have been interested in and concerned about the case, were entirely unaware of it due to the poor performance of the Canadian media, which took no interest in the story until after it had become front page news in the United States. Even then it was downplayed and ignored in many parts of the country.

It seems then that Canadian decision-makers at every juncture concluded that no special effort was required of them. Who that mattered would care about their failure to act? The murder victim was, after all, poor, Indian, female and politically radical; she was also idealistic, energetic, capable and committed to her people's fight for equal rights and self-determination. Because the sacrifice of her rights weakens our own and because her vision and efforts enriched our world, however, many people will care about what happened to Anna Mae Aquash.

Afterword

My sister's murderer, or murderers, will probably never be found. I believe the person or persons responsible may be connected with the FBI, perhaps not directly but indirectly somehow. Anna died as a result of ignorance on the part of the killers: she was one person against many of them. Who could she have hurt? They say the FBI is the most powerful body in the United States. Nobody can get near it. How could she have hurt it?

Anna was an educated person—a person with common sense. She worked for the American Indian Movement out of dedication, not for publicity or headlines. The real Indian people, those who are like her, should be controlling that movement.

My sister's death has taught me to foretell the events that will take place in this country. I have learned—from all she told me—to see what is happening. The same things will happen here as have happened in the United States. This country will become another South Dakota.

Mary Lafford

Sources

Chapter 1

The interviews and personal observations of journalist Kevin McKiernan have been used extensively in the preparation of this book. McKiernan spent more than three years reporting on the American Indian Movement. Tapes of his broadcasts are available from Minnesota Public Radio, 400 Sibly Avenue, St. Paul, Minnesota. Unless otherwise noted, information in this book is based on primary sources researched by McKiernan and the author, including interviews with Pine Ridge Reservation residents, police officials and family, friends and associates of Anna Mae Aquash in the United States and Canada.

The issue of criminal investigation and jurisdiction on the reservation requires some explanation. On the reservation, the FBI has jurisdiction over 13 major crimes, which include murder, rape, felonious assault and arson. The Bureau of Indian Affairs (BIA) police, who are native people recruited from the reservation, investigate minor crimes. The Sioux feel that the FBI's presence on the reservation is a violation of their treaty rights, a position that was upheld in the early 1880s when the U.S. Supreme Court agreed that the federal government had no authority over reservation crime. The Seven Major Crimes Act of 1885 first made reservation Indians subject to federal law.

In 1976-77 the law enforcement system on Pine Ridge Reservation underwent significant changes as a result of abuses during previous administrations. Today there are no BIA police as such. Local law enforcement officers are hired by each reservation district and are overseen by a police commission made up of district representatives as well as Pine Ridge village residents. Law enforcement is no longer centred in Pine Ridge village as it was during the years when the events described in this chapter took place.

Chapter 2

This chapter is based on the experiences of Kevin McKiernan, who spent several weeks inside Wounded Knee and covered the occupation both before and after government-imposed controls denied reporters access to the occupied village. His experiences form the basis for the account of news management in this chapter. Some of his observations of the Wounded Knee occupation were published in the December 31, 1974 issue of *The Minnesota Leader*, Minneapolis, Minnesota.

Voices From Wounded Knee, published by *Akwasasne Notes*, an international native peoples newspaper (Mohawk Nation at Akwasasne, via Rooseveltown, New York), provides the best account of the Wounded Knee occupation and is based on the experiences of participants. It includes details about Pentagon involvement during the occupation.

Further accounts of Pentagon coordination of federal troops during the siege can be found in "Garden Plot—'Flowers of Evil'," *Akwasasne Notes*, early winter 1975, p. 6ff.; "Bringing Vietnam Home," *Akwasasne Notes*, early winter 1975, p. 4ff. and "Garden Plot and Swat, U.S. Police as New Action Enemy" by Tim Butz, *Counterspy*, fall 1974 (P.O. Box 647, Ben Franklin Station, Washington D.C.).

Events leading up to the occupation are described in *The Road to Wounded Knee* by Robert Burnette and John Koster (New York: Bantam, 1974), which is valuable for its historical presentation of abuses on the reservation. Health and income statistics used in this chapter are also drawn from *The Road to Wounded*

Knee, p. 71ff. The role of the BIA on the reservation described in this chapter is based on Kevin McKiernan's interviews with numerous native people. His tape "Voices from the Reservation" is available from Minnesota Public Radio. *The Road to Wounded Knee* (p. 178ff.) is also pertinent here. The actions of tribal chairman Richard Wilson which resulted in the occupation of Wounded Knee are documented in *Voices from Wounded Knee* (p. 10-33), *The Road to Wounded Knee* (p. 220ff.) and McKiernan's tape "Voices from the Reservation".

BIA, I'm Not Your Indian Anymore (Rooseveltown, N.Y.: *Akwasasne Notes*, 1972) is an account of the 1972 Trail of Broken Treaties Caravan based on news reports and observations of participants. Historical material on the 1890 massacre at Wounded Knee is based on *Bury My Heart at Wounded Knee: An Indian History of the American West* by Dee Brown (New York: Holt, Rinehart & Winston, 1971).

An eyewitness account of the murder of Byron De Sersa is available on tape from Minnesota Public Radio ("The Murder of Byron De Sersa").

The quotation "I am a woman who is forced...." is from a letter sent to Kevin McKiernan and published in *The Minnesota Leader*, September 1, 1975.

Chapter 3

Material on Anna Mae Aquash's early life was gathered from her family and friends in Nova Scotia, Massachusetts and elsewhere.

Chapter 4

Information in this chapter is based on the final report of the U.S. Senate Select Committee on Intelligence, chaired by Senator Frank Church. A copy of the report is available from the U.S. Government Printing Office, Washington, D.C.

Additional information comes from a host of newspaper articles reporting on legal action taken by the Socialist Workers Party and by the family and friends of Black Panther leaders Mark Clark and Fred Hampton. Some of the documents released by the FBI as a result of the SWP suit have been reprinted in *COINTELPRO: The FBI's Secret War on Freedom* edited by Nelson Blackstock (New York: Monad Press, 1976). See also "COINTELPRO: How the FBI Tried to Destroy the Black Panthers" by Sid Blumenthal, *Canadian Dimension*, January 1975.

Chapter 5

Information in this chapter is based on the observations and research of Kevin McKiernan. His tape "Wounded Knee Trial Epilogue" is available from Minnesota Public Radio.

Senator Frank Church is quoted from his testimony at the trial of Darelle Butler and Robert Robideau in Cedar Rapids, Iowa, July 9, 1976. This testimony was published in the late autumn 1976 issue of *Akwasasne Notes*.

Statistical data on the Wounded Knee cases and arrests may be found in "Fair and Equal Justice" by Kenneth Tilsen, *Quare* (the student newspaper of the University of Minnesota Law School), September 1976.

It has not been possible to detail the full scope of the FBI campaign against the American Indian Movement. To do so would be a book in itself. However, details of attacks similar to COINTELPRO are contained in almost every issue of *Akwasasne Notes* published since the occupation of Wounded Knee (see especially the early winter 1975 issue). The "Dog Soldier" teletype was published in "Who Are the Real Terorists?" *Akwasasne Notes*, late fall 1976, p. 4ff. See also "The FBI War Game and the NWT" in *Native Press*, November 12, 1976, p. 1 (Box 1992, Yellowknife, NWT). The Minnesota Citizens' Review Commission on the FBI held hearings in March 1977 and outlined the scope of the FBI campaign against native Americans. The commission report is available from the Minnesota Church Centre, Room 220, 122 West Franklin Avenue, Minneapolis, Minnesota.

Chapter 6

Details of Douglass Durham's past life were revealed by him in twelve hours of taped interviews with AIM attorneys and independent observers. AIM subsequently published a pamphlet entitled *Anatomy of an Informer*, which is available from the AIM National Office, White Earth Reservation, Minnesota. Other accounts of Durham's activities, based largely on these tapes, include "Anatomy of an Informer," *Akwasasne Notes*, early summer 1975, p. 14; "Anatomy of an Informer—Part II," *Akwasasne Notes*, early winter 1975, p. 10ff. and "Wounded Knee Trials Go On—The Invisible Man in Phoenix and an FBI Behind Every Mailbox," *Akwasasne Notes*, early spring 1975, p. 30ff. Durham's account of his activities in AIM are also contained in the report of Senator James Eastland's subcommittee on internal security entitled "Revolutionary Activities within the United States, The American Indian Movement". The report is available from the U.S. Government Printing Office, Washington, D.C.

Additional information on Durham is included in "Secret Agent Douglass Durham and the Death of Jancita Eagle Deer" by Paula Giese in the March-April 1976 issue of *North Country Anvil* (P.O. Box 37, Millville, Minnesota). Giese's article outlines how Durham was able to manipulate the young woman and how he was able to locate her after the complaints of the Rosebud Sioux in fall 1974.

President Gerald Ford established a commission of inquiry to investigate the domestic spying program of the CIA on January 5, 1975, after details of such a program were revealed in *The New York Times*. The commission report was summarized in the June 11, 1975 issue of the *Times*, pp. 18-20. The limited findings of the commission, headed by Vice-President Nelson Rockefeller, were subject to considerable criticism.

"The Occupation of Anicinabe Park" by John Gallagher and Cy Gonick, *Canadian Dimension*, November 1974, details events of that protest. "Welcome to Ottawa, The Native People's Caravan" by David Ticoll and Stan Persky, *Canadian Dimension*, January 1975, is a more coherent description of the caravan than provided in various news reports.

The FBI and Douglass Durham's involvement in the Sky-horse-Mohawk case is discussed in "The FBI Takes Aim at AIM" by Elliott Kanter, *Seven Days*, April 11, 1977 and in "Skyhorse-Mohawk Trial," *Akwasasne Notes*, early spring 1977, p. 16 and "Judge Finds Trial Humorous," *Akwasasne Notes*, early summer 1976, p. 8ff.

William Janklow's statement about the best way to deal with AIM leaders was made prior to his election as state attorney general in 1974 and was published after Dennis Banks referred to the statement during an appearance on the NBC *Today* show. An Associated Press report was published in the March 23, 1976 issue of the Aberdeen, South Dakota *American News* and elsewhere. The original statement was contained in a sworn affadavit.

Chapter 7

This chapter is based on interviews with relatives, friends and associates of Anna Mae Aquash in St. Paul-Minneapolis, Ottawa, Boston and the Pine Ridge Reservation.

Information on the reign of terror in Pine Ridge during early 1975 can also be found in "Pine Ridge after Wounded Knee: The Terror Goes On," *Akwasasne Notes*, early summer 1975, p. 8ff.

Chapter 8

There are numerous reports of the June 26, 1975 shoot-out. The account in this chapter is based largely on the observations of Kevin McKiernan, who was on the reservation during the gun battle. He was among the reporters who entered the shoot-out site immediately after the incident. This chapter includes his observations of the body of Joe Stuntz. Other reports of the shoot-out include "Death in Oglala," *Akwasasne Notes*, late summer 1975, p. 4ff. and "Two FBI Men Die, Indian Slain" by John Crewdson, *The New York Times*, June 27, 1975, p. 1.

An account of the Oregon interstate highway incident is contained in "The Government's Secret War Against the Indians" by Tom Bates, *Oregon Times Magazine*, February-March 1976. The description used in this chapter is based on an itnerview with Kenneth Loudhawk and on information made public during the 1977 trial of Leonard Peltier in Fargo, North Dakota.

The Butler-Robideau trial is discussed in "Open Fire, or the FBI's History Lesson" by Judy Gumbo Clavir and Stew Albert, *Crawdaddy*, November 1976.

A transcript of Anna Mae Aquash's account of the September 5 raid on the home of Al Running was published in the June 1976 issue of *Indian Voice* (201-423 West Broadway, Vancouver, British Columbia). Pierre attorney Robert Riter was appointed by the court to represent Anna Mae Aquash in this case because WKLDOC attorney Bruce Ellison, who would normally have defended her, was not able to do so. Ellison maintains that after he successfully passed the South Dakota bar examination, his bar card was withheld for ten weeks, during which time he was unable to appear in court. Charges against Anna Mae Aquash's co-defendants in the September 5 raid and in the November 14 Oregon interstate highway incident were later dismissed.

Chapter 9

Banks' statement about the AIM investigation of the death of Anna Mae Aquash is contained in "The Killing of Anna Mae Aquash" by David Weir and Lowell Briggman, *Rolling Stone*, April 7, 1977, p. 54. This article also contains some of the suspicions about John Stewart. Other information is from personal interviews with individuals on Pine Ridge Reservation. Stewart denied he was an informer in a letter to the editor of *Akwasasne Notes*, early summer 1976, p. 47.

Chapter 10

This chapter includes information based on two news articles: "The Strange Killing of a Wounded Knee Indian" by Jerry Oppenheimer, *The Washington Star*, May 24, 1976, p. 1 and "Indian Woman's Death Raises Many Questions" by Kevin McKiernan, *The Minneapolis Tribune*, May 30, 1976. An analysis of the press coverage of the Aquash case can be found in *Content*, June 1976 and July 1976.

Questions and answers heard in the Canadian House of Commons are recorded in Hansard under the following dates in 1976: April 29, May 31, June 29, November 15 and December 22.

Douglass Durham's testimony before the Eastland Committee is outlined in "Indians Smuggle Arms over U.S.-Canada Line, FBI Man Says," *The Toronto Globe and Mail*, September 18, 1976, p. 1. Information on the St. Regis Reserve incident is in "One of a Series of Events Here," *Akwasasne Notes*, early winter 1975, p. 2. See also "The Riddle of Nelson Small Legs" by Marci MacDonald, *Maclean's*, October 18, 1976, p. 26ff. and "Keeping an Ear on Labour and the Left" by Caroline Brown, *Canadian Dimension*, June 1976, p. 2.

Information on allegations of RCMP wrongdoing is contained in "The Mounties: It's Just One Damn (or Damnable) Thing After Another," *Maclean's*, November 28, 1977, pp. 17-19, and in the almost daily reports of *The Toronto Globe and Mail*, including "RCMP Distributed Private OHIP Data to Disrupt Extremists," November 14, 1977, p. 1 and "Some Political Groups Shadowed by OPP," November 2, 1977, p. 1. See also Hansard, particularly October 31, 1977, for Parliamentary discussions of RCMP misconduct.